The

Modern Woman's

Guide

to an

Old Fashioned

Christmas

How to make it stress-free!

by Betsy Watson

Check out our website at
www.christmashousepublishing.com

This title is also available as an ebook

Published by Christmas House Publishing, Inc.
P.O. Box 1845
Newport, Arkansas, 72112

ISBN: 099043690x
ISBN - 13: 978-0-9904369-0-4

Library of Congress Control Number: 2014909575

Christmas House Publishing, Inc.
Newport, AR

Contents

Introduction
    "I'm Dreaming of a White Christmas!"

Chapter One: PLANNING
    "It's Beginning to Feel a Lot Like Christmas!"

Chapter Two: DECORATING
    "So Ring Those Christmas Bells!"

Chapter Three: GIFTS and CARDS
    "In the Days of Auld Lang Syne!"

Chapter Four: COOKING
    "Christmas Is Coming, the Goose Is Getting Fat!"

Chapter Five: ENTERTAINING
    "We Need a Little Christmas Now!"

Chapter Six: TAMING STRESS
    "You'd Better Not Pout!"

Chapter Seven: AFTER CHRISTMAS
    "On the Twelfth Day of Christmas . . ."

FOR FURTHER READING

Introduction

"I'm Dreaming of a White Christmas!"

Christmas is a magical time, and we all want to fall under its spell. Twinkling lights, gifts under the tree, hot chocolate by a roaring fire – all are images of joy and contentment, and all remind us of a quieter, lovelier day when life moved at a slower pace, when friends and family had more time for each other, and when our wants and needs were simpler, less expensive, and ultimately, more satisfying. How can we recapture those gracious pleasures in a fragmented world of smart phones, computer games, and over-filled calendars? How can we create such cherished experiences and memories when women's lives are so much busier than they used to be?

As a veteran of many, many years of Christmas-making, I have written this book as a "how-to" guide for young women who yearn for a beautiful Christmas season and yet feel daunted by the prospect of having to create it. I have been there! I can help you make it happen! I will walk you through every stage of the process so that by the end of the season you will be well on your way toward building your own Christmas traditions.

Part cookbook, part weekly planner, part advice column, this little book is a collection of "notes-to-self" I have compiled over many years in my own Christmas notebook. You will have to find your own craft projects, your own decorating tips, and your own sources for great gifts, but if you will take me along I will steer you clear of many of the pitfalls that await the novice Christmas-creator. And I promise you we will have fun along the way!

I have been "doing Christmas" for more years than I care to admit. Just to be totally honest, I am a Christmas nut! I love everything about the holiday season, and I have tried to do most of it at one time or another over the last forty years. (My mother produced a very sensible, under-stated holiday celebration when my brothers and I were growing up, and the child in me has always yearned for lots of sparkle, festivity, entertaining, and food!) For the last twenty years I have kept a red Christmas notebook close at hand from September through January, and I have developed for myself a number of guidelines and principles that keep me from having to reinvent the wheel every year. It finally occurred to me that my red notebook could probably be helpful to lots of other folks who don't have time to experiment in all the ways I have done over the years, and the book you are holding in your hands is the product of that flash of insight and inspiration. I wrote it for my nieces, cousins, and future daughters-in-law, but if you are looking for help in planning your own holiday, I hope it will be the roadmap *you* need to set out on your journey and arrive safely at your destination.

My advice to you is to pick and choose from the areas I outline in this book, and then add some ideas of your own. Choose the things that speak to your heart and that will create the experiences that have the most meaning for you. You can't do it all, so what is most important to you *this year*? Will it be ornaments and the tree? cooking Christmas Dinner? decorating the house (inside and out)? entertaining? gift buying and wrapping? Decide what you want to learn, accomplish, concentrate-on this year, and let the rest go. This is a *process*, and your Christmases will *grow* with you. You will have many years to master all the arts of creating Christmas and making it shine in your memory as a source of great joy and pleasure.

Try to remember that it does not have to be perfect. This is a life-long learning experience, and you will get better at it each year. In the meantime, hold in your heart the reason we are celebrating. As the inestimable Charles Dickens had Scrooge's nephew say to the old humbug:

"*I have always thought of Christmas time, when it has come round . . . as a good time: a kind, forgiving, charitable, pleasant time: the only time I know of, in the long calendar of the year, when men and women seem by one consent to open their shut-up hearts freely, and to think of people below them as if they really were fellow-passengers to the grave, and not another race of creatures bound on other journeys. And therefore uncle, though it has never put a scrap of gold or silver in my pocket, I believe that it* has *done me good, and* will *do me good; and I say, God bless it!*"

~ ~ Charles Dickens,
A <u>Christmas</u> <u>Carol</u>

Ah, Christmas is coming. **Oh my goodness, we have a lot to do! Let's get started!**

Chapter One
PLANNING

"It's Beginning to Feel a Lot Like Christmas!"

Oh, the magic of Christmas! Everyone wants to be a part of it! But as wonderful as it all is, there is no getting around the fact that the Christmas-making process requires a lot of work, and we can easily wear ourselves out if we attempt too much. So let's figure out how to create a holiday celebration for our friends and families that is both magic and **manageable**.

Start with the things that are most important to you *this year*, and plan around that. Next year you can add one or two new areas of expertise, then more the year after that. The important thing is to keep it as simple as possible while you learn the ropes, so you and the people around you can enjoy the season.

Some stress is inevitable, but if you are finding yourself stressed out all the time, you are attempting too much. Remember that you are striving for a happy, peaceful season for yourself as well as for your family and friends, and frazzled is not where you want to be. And you don't want to head into the New Year with your energies depleted, especially if you have to go back to work! Above all, try to remember that the real purpose of the season is to prepare our hearts for the arrival in the world of hope, peace and joy, and you can't do that if you are frantic and exhausted.

Now let's get real: as I've already said, Christmas is a lot of work, and <u>you</u> are the one who is going to have to do it. It is a fantasy to think that your husband-children-friends are going to help you. They won't, so just get over it – and plan accordingly. Plan what <u>you</u> can manage. The operative word here is PLAN.

The Christmas magic *will* come, and you can savor it and lose yourself in the wonder and creativity of it, if you have <u>prepared</u> <u>in</u> <u>advance</u>. Do as much as you can long before the season arrives:

<u>Plan</u> (and preferably buy) your gifts – and buy the boxes, wrapping paper, tissue, scotch tape, and *batteries* before Thanksgiving. Do *not* get stuck at the mall looking for gifts after the tenth of December; that is a formula for disaster, and you will waste precious time and money. Visiting the mall can be fun and festive *after* your major gift decisions have already been made and executed.

<u>Plan</u> your decorations – Will it be a full-size tree? Do you want wreaths on the doors? Do you know where you can buy these things? If you already have them, who will help you get them out of the attic or the storage room? Will you need help getting the tree in the stand, and if so, who can you call?

<u>Plan</u> your entertaining - Will you be cooking Christmas Dinner? Do you want to have a party? Will you be expected to plan room parties at your children's schools? Will you need to contribute dishes for pot-lucks at the church, office or school?

<u>Plan</u> your menus – What will you serve at that luncheon for six ladies you've always thought would be fun? What would make a nice Christmas morning brunch for your family and friends? What are some easy meals you can feed your family when the holiday demands get really pressing?

And always, *always*, guard against planning too much. You can't do it all every year! Decide in October what you want to attempt this year, <u>then</u> <u>stick</u> <u>to</u> <u>your</u> <u>plan</u>. Christmas *can* seem very daunting, but you can do it! It all depends on putting yourself in control and then not getting carried away.

You'll be tempted to try to do more when the spirit of the season ensnares you, but as my financial planner brother says: "Plan your work and then work your plan." Try to remember that you only have a limited amount of creative energy, and time, and if you attempt too much, you'll burn out. Let your family identify with you the things they want to do and see done, and then let the rest go. If you get to the point that it stops being fun, STOP! Go to bed. Get some rest. It will be fun again tomorrow. And if it's not, you probably don't need to be doing it.

If you are new to this Christmas business, just know at the outset that you'll have to make choices. In getting started, focus on the tree, the gifts, and Christmas Dinner. Then you can add more things next year, if time allows.

First decision: will you buy a live **tree** or an artificial one? Either way, there is a lot to learn: how to keep it alive, how to put on the lights, how to keep the baby from pulling it over, how to make it look "full" when you can't afford many ornaments. We'll talk about all of those things and more in later chapters.

Buy your **gifts** far in advance, preferably on sale, and stick with them. The best marketing minds in America are out there trying to get you to buy their products, and if you don't have a game plan you'll just be frustrated, and you'll spend too much.

Where are you going to have **Christmas Dinner**? If it's at your house, what are you going to serve, and who can help out with the cooking? If it's at someone else's house, how can you help them?

The key to all of this is to get *organized*. Buy a <u>red</u> three-ring binder, a set of tabbed dividers, a set of pocket folders, some wide-ruled lined paper, and a three-hole puncher. Label dividers for September, October, November, December and January. These sections will tell you what needs to be accomplished along the way to stay on track. Also include sections for Gifts, Needs for Next Year, and Reflections. You can save recipes and newspaper articles in the pocket folders. Now you're ready to get started.

Keep notes to yourself – in your notebook - all through the season. You will have dozens of inspirations and epiphanies along the way, and you will **not** remember all these details and insights by next year. If you have written them down, they will be enormously helpful to you when you start your planning next September. There's no need to start from scratch every year! Very little will happen as planned, but your notebook will become your guide to what needs to get done.

Buy or make a large planning calendar for the month of December, and **pencil-in** your plans and obligations as they become clear to you. After Thanksgiving, move your large calendar into the kitchen where you can see it and make needed changes every day. This visual cue will help to keep you on track and make you aware of how fast the season is moving. After Christmas, save your calendar in your notebook. This will be a tremendous help to you next year as you start your planning.

If you are just starting to develop your own Christmas traditions, you can't be completely organized this year, but you can Start Now!

Okay, let's just admit it right up front – Christmas is expensive. And if you let yourself get carried away by the spirit of the season, it can be *very expensive*. We're not just talking gifts here; we're talking decorations, cards, clothes, food, and entertaining. We're back to our Number One Principle: you have to plan!

What does all this mean? It means you have to start *saving* way before December. Every month, set aside a few dollars for your Christmas expenses. Have a garage sale in the summer, then save the money for Christmas. Work overtime a few weekends and – you guessed it – save the money for Christmas. Hit the end-of-season sales all through the year and buy presents for cousins, neighbors, teachers, co-workers, your lunch bunch, you children's friends, etc. It's amazing what you can find on half-of-half (75% off) if you are vigilant. You do not have to buy "the perfect gift" for each recipient; most gifts can just be tasty or useful reminders that you care about that person and want to add to their holiday joy.

Whatever you do, do <u>not</u> charge your Christmas expenses to a credit card. It is just so easy to whip that little piece of plastic out there – which somehow doesn't feel like you are spending money at all.

When you get caught up in the magic of the season you can spend way more money than your sensible self would have approved under different circumstances. Once again, if you take charge of your Christmas *in advance* and make careful plans, you can avoid this most distressing of all the Christmas pitfalls. You do not want to start the new year with a depressingly large total on your credit card bill!

Above all else, through this overly busy season take control of your emotions. When panic starts to set in (and it will) tame it into submission with deep breaths and positive affirmations: "I CAN get this done. I DO have enough time. I AM going to enjoy creating this happy season for my family and friends, and for ME!" Remember, this is a learning experience, and you will get better at it each year. In the meantime, try to remember also that the whole point is to prepare a place in your heart for the coming of the new hope that is about to be born into the world.

Here are my suggestions, month by month, for how to plan ahead and make Christmas work.

September:

Think about a picture for your Christmas card, if you plan to send them. Did you get a good picture at the beach last summer? How about pictures from the kids' birthday parties? Can you get a neighbor to capture a shot of the whole family doing something together? Make your decision about sending Christmas cards and choose that picture.

Make sure your address list is up-to-date (for the cards and the thank-you notes). Track down all those address this month!

Review your gift list, decide what you already have and what you need to buy or make, and start filling in the gaps.

October:

Schedule all of your appointments such as mammogram, pap smear, teeth cleaning, oil change, and get them out of the way before Thanksgiving.

Make a list of all needed household maintenance – window washing, leaf raking, putting away the hoses – and plan to accomplish all before Thanksgiving.

Buy your gift wrap, ribbon, tags, Scotch Tape, Elmer's Glue, and *batteries*.

Order your cards if you are sending them, and print out your address labels.

Make decisions about catalog orders for gifts, and place the orders.

Decide <u>with</u> <u>thought</u> <u>and</u> <u>care</u> what activities and projects you want to attempt this Christmas. Record them in your notebook. Resolve to let the rest go.

November: (November is the key to making it all work!)

Make your large December calendar for the kitchen. All through November, check and revise your December planning calendar as invitations and obligations crop up (as they will, many of them unexpectedly).

Cook ahead and freeze any portions you can of Christmas Dinner, Christmas Eve Dinner, Christmas morning brunch, or other cooking obligations you can anticipate – so you won't have to be in the kitchen while your family is having fun in December. Also cook ahead and have several December at-home meals in the freezer for your family, and don't forget breakfasts for when the kids are out of school. It's no fun to be stuck in the kitchen while your family is watching Christmas movies and sipping hot chocolate in the den!

Finish your Christmas gift shopping and have as many things as possible gift-wrapped at the store (I try to shop where the wrapping is free). Do as much of the gift-wrapping as possible, and the boxing, if the package needs to be mailed. Looking for the right size of cardboard boxes at the last minute inevitably leads to stress.

Have your Christmas cards printed or signed, stuffed, and addressed *before Thanksgiving* (though you won't drop them in the mail until about December 10th).

Figure out where you are going to move your regular decorative items when you get out your Christmas treasures, and clear a space where you can take them in another part of the house. **Do *not*** let them become clutter in any of your heavily-traveled living areas.

Buy note paper and stamps for writing your Christmas thank you notes – and also for the children to do theirs. Put them away where you plan to store your off-season household decorations.

If you are going to do any entertaining over the holidays, figure out your Christmas table centerpiece *before Thanksgiving*. That can be a source of extreme stress, especially when you try to do it at the last minute – and inevitably you will not be able to find the little finishing touches you will want to use. If the centerpiece is decided in advance, you can enjoy the creativity of gussying-up the rest of your table, and that's one of the real pleasures of the holidays.

Do NOT have Thanksgiving and Christmas Dinners both at your house! The cooking and the decorating will exhaust you.

Locate your Christmas clothes and jewelry and get all in good wearing order. Figure out what else you need. Except for very fancy occasions, all you really need is black pants, a black turtle neck or good long-sleeved t-shirt, a red jacket or sweater, a couple of Christmas necklaces (a silver snowflake goes anywhere), a couple of Christmas scarves, black boots and heels, and perhaps a sparkly vest. (Remember the stockings, tights or socks!) A jewel-tone dress with a statement necklace would make your Christmas wardrobe just about perfect.

The last week in November is crucial to a stress-free Christmas. Get the Thanksgiving decorations put away and make sure your house is clean and orderly. (It probably won't be that way again until after New Year's!) I have been known to put up my tree on Thanksgiving weekend, especially if I am having a Christmas party.

December:

Your planning calendar and notebook are the keys to making the season work. Use them like your Bible.

It is absolutely certain that things will come up in December you had no way to anticipate: the dishwasher breaks; the shower leaks and you need a carpenter; something goes wrong and you have to go to the doctor – where you WILL have a long wait; you catch a cold while delivering your gifts in the rain; you have a flat and the tire needs to be replaced; the disposal gets clogged and you have to call a plumber; the satellite TV man has to come and you have to wait for him. Do not fill your calendar so full that you don't have any flexibility. This causes Stress with a capital S!

You will have to be very flexible with your calendar – you will rarely be able to accomplish all the things you have listed for any given day. Just review at the end of each day and move items over as need be.

Keep it simple, and make it fun. You're creating memories for yourself and your family, so focus on the simple pleasures of doing things together, playing lots of Christmas music, and keeping good smells wafting through the house – either from baking, or scented candles, or potpourri.

Remember that the regular things of your life – cooking dinner, doing the wash, running carpools, going to meetings, going to work – will continue through the holiday season. Don't try to pack in too much. You have many years to build your traditions and master the techniques.

Restrain yourself on your decorating. Remember that you are going to have to take it all down and put it away, and putting it away properly is a huge undertaking that will take just as long as getting it out – and it's a lot less fun!

Don't drag all the decorations out at once. Those messy boxes sitting around become too oppressive; just decorate one area at a time.

Set up a wrapping area that will work both for you and the kids – it can be as simple as a card table in an area that doesn't get much use. Stock it with Scotch Tape, scissors, gift tags, pens, wrapping paper, and ribbon. Give the kids a few pointers on how to fold the corners and tie the bows, then let them do their own wrapping. They'll love it, and they'll be proud of their creations.

Do Not Rush. That is the worst thing you can do to deplete your energy. A wise friend of mine used to say "Hurry is not the work of the Devil. Hurry IS the Devil." Slow down, take deep breaths, and stay calm. Just don't goof off . . . there's no time for that! If you find yourself getting stressed out, cut back on what you are attempting.

Do some kind of Advent reading every day. I like to do it early in the morning while the house is quiet and before the rush of that day's plans takes over. It will remind you of why we are celebrating, and it will help you stay calm.

Decorate early, and finish by the 10th. Clean up your messes as you go, and do not let the clutter of boxes and unused decorations accumulate – they will become very oppressive!

Wear rubber gloves while you do the dishes. I have discovered a wonderful product in the Vermont Country Store catalog. It's Lotil cream, and it works like a charm on cracked and hurting finger tips. Wear rubber gloves and you won't have to buy it!

Put a jar of hand and cuticle cream beside your bed and use it every night. Those hands get chapped with all the dishwashing, cooking, and decorating you will do.

Wear a coat! You don't have time to get sick.

If you are sending cards, put them in the mail by December 10th. Then make corrections to your address list as cards from friends start to arrive. If you don't have time to stop and work on your address list each day, at least save the envelopes so you can do it after the holidays.

Deliver your gifts as early as possible – you guessed it, by the 10th. Keep the gifts simple and have them wrapped at the store.

For kids' gifts, try to have something that moves – and be sure to buy the batteries.

Unless you (or your children) love to see the gifts accumulating under the tree, open YOUR presents as they come in and write the thank you notes. This is one of the best gifts you can give yourself, because there is so much to do after Christmas that you won't feel like sitting down to write notes.

By this time things will be getting hectic, and the planning you have done in advance will become of paramount importance. You will not have time to think – you'll need to go on autopilot. Be sure to make notes for next year all through the holidays. Enjoy the next two weeks, and let it be magic!

Christmas Day – record the gifts from friends and relatives as they are opened. Put the list in your red notebook.

The day after Christmas, attend the half-of-half sales and buy for next Christmas. (Your kids will be busy playing with their new toys, and there are no better left-overs than Christmas Dinner!) Bring home all your treasures, spread them out on the living room floor, and make your decisions about who gets what next year. *Put the list in your Christmas notebook.* Box the gifts and put them away where they will be protected from heat and cold for the next year (not in the attic or the rented storage room).

On December 28th start your kids *and you* writing your thank-you notes, and do five a day. All you really need to say is "thank you for the _____. I really appreciate your thoughtfulness, and it will remind me of you every time I see it. We had a wonderful Christmas, and we hope you did too."

Start taking down the decorations and do it all neatly. Repair any broken pieces. If possible, put things away in the room they will go in. Do not get in a hurry. Do one area at a time and then put it away, so you can avoid the oppressive clutter of having half-filled boxes everywhere. I like to take the tree down last, because I hate to see it go.

January:

Get the last vestiges of your decorations put away as quickly, and neatly, as possible.

Finish any un-written thank-you notes.

Watch the sales for next year's gifts for neighbors, cousins, teachers, co-workers, etc., and also for good artificial greenery, wrapping paper you really like, and holiday clothing items that you realized during the season you needed.

Review your Christmas notebook and fill it in with insights and inspirations from this year.

Put away your Christmas notebook in a place that you can retrieve it easily when you have inspirations or purchase gifts through the year. That's why it is RED – in July you will not be in a Christmas frame of mind, and if your notebook is not obvious and in an accessible place, you will not record these notes. Remember, organization is the key!

Whew! Okay ladies, this is a lot of work, but it is oh, so much fun. And the pay-off comes years later when your family is sitting around together some holiday in the future talking about the good old days and someone says "Remember that Christmas when [very proper] Aunt Mildred put on the blond wig and came dancing into the den?" and then someone else says, "How about the time [very shy] Uncle Bill put on sunglasses and crooned 'Blue Christmas', and [our little dog] Millie started to howl?" And you realize that they really were paying attention, and they really did love it. And then they want to learn how to make Uncle Elbert's Eggnog for YOU, and they surprise you by making the Mini Blinies for Christmas Brunch and slipping them into the freezer while you are out shopping for groceries. All of a sudden you know that your family has traditions that they cherish, and you really did make it magic for them. It doesn't get much better than that.

Despite all the blaring messages of our excessively consumerist culture, the season of Christmas does not actually start until December 25th. Remember "The Twelve Days of Christmas?" with the five gold rings and the partridge in a pear tree? Those twelve days go from December 25th to January 6th! The month before that is the season of Advent in the church calendar – a season of preparation for the birth of Christ, supposedly a season of quiet and contemplation, a season of self-examination, meditation and reflection. Those goals are increasingly hard to accomplish in the media-driven world of the 21st century, but I encourage you to buy a book of Advent readings and start each day with a quiet reminder of why we are celebrating. It will calm your frazzled nerves, it will focus your attention on what is important, and it will send you out into the world with a renewed sense of the joy that is at the heart of Christmas.

So let's get started on creating *your* wonderful holiday.

Chapter Two
DECORATING

"So Ring Those Christmas Bells!"

Oh, I do love to decorate! Nothing gets me in the spirit faster than throwing open my Christmas cabinets and thinking about where to place all my treasures. I have the good fortune to live in a house with lots of storage spaces, so the Christmas decorations can come marching out in an organized fashion, room by room. And I need all those cabinets because I have been collecting loved pieces for many, many years.

You will collect your own treasures, too, but right at the outset I want to encourage you to make your purchases very carefully and don't overdo it. That will be hard, because there are so many cute and wonderful things on the market in the late fall, but try to think of your purchases as investments, and remember that your tastes will change over the years.

Remember too that everything you buy has to be *stored* for eleven months of the year. So get a grip on your enthusiasm, and let's approach this decorating business in an organized fashion.

What are your priorities this year? Of course you will probably want a tree, whether large or small. And you'll want some kind of greenery on the front door and elsewhere. You'll need a centerpiece for your dining table, and festive placemats and napkins. Do you need something on the buffet and mantel? What about the coffee table? The front hall? The stairs? The first order of business is to *plan it*, then go out in search of your supplies armed with this information. Let the stores and malls spark your imagination, but try not to buy little decorative items at this stage of the game. Just enjoy looking!

THE TREE

Of course, the tree comes first. What is Christmas without a tree? That doesn't mean it has to be a BIG tree – little trees can be charming, and if you have the room to store them you can put them away *decorated* and use them year after year. I have a small, pre-lit funky one that always goes on my front hall table. Something like this would work very well in an apartment or if you need to keep little folks from pulling it over.

And then again there is the lure of the big tree. Mine goes up on the first of December (sometimes before!) and it casts its magic over the whole house. It takes up a corner of the den and goes all the way to the ceiling (after the angel or the star or the big red bow goes on top). Often on December nights we turn off all the other lights and just sit in the dark gazing at our twinkling, magical tree, enchanted by its beauty and savoring all the pleasures of the season. What IS in all those packages? How much longer do we have to wait to find out? Anything under there from Tiffany's? Ha!

For years I thought nothing would do but a live tree. I spent a small fortune every Christmas buying a Canadian Balsam and then, with hired help, wrestled it into the very large stand it required. One year the darned thing fell over, and I paid two men by the hour to stand around doing nothing while I raced to Walmart to buy a bigger stand. You guessed it, I had to wait in a long line to check out. That was just one of the inevitable glitches of the season.

Live trees just smell so very good, and if you think you have to have one, here are a few tips. Do not bring it in the house before December 10th, and then plan to take it down on December 26th. By then it will be completely dried out and it will be a fire hazard. When you are ready to bring it in the house, saw off an inch or so from the bottom, snip off enough of the bottom branches to make it fit securely

in the holder, and save those snipped-off pieces to use in your decorating. Do not let the newly-cut portion of the tree touch the ground! If it does, the sap will re-seal the bottom, and it will not drink water. Once you have it in the stand, add warm water, and it will drink heavily at first. Add sugar-water every day – one cup of sugar per gallon of water – or buy one of the commercially available tree life extenders and use it instead. Even with conscientious watering, the tree will drop needles and make a fine mess. As it dries out, it will also release the spores that are sealed in the needles, so if you are at all prone to allergies you should wear a mask while you put it up and take it down.

Many different kinds of trees are available all over the country, and it can be a great family adventure to go out and cut one in the woods, or to choose one in a gaily-lit Christmas tree lot. Probably the favorites are the Douglas Fir, which is shaped like a pyramid and very bushy (smells good and holds its needles well), the Noble or Fraser Firs, which show off ornaments well, and the ever-popular and always-available Scotch Pine, which may be a bit sticky and prickly. Many other varieties are available, and many of them can be purchased in a container with the root-ball attached, then later planted in the yard. These trees can only stay in the house for about a week, in a sunny and cool spot. If you go with the container choice, place a few ice cubes on top of the ball periodically to keep it moist.

Putting on the lights is an art in itself, and done properly it is very labor-intensive, easily taking three or four hours. My husband had no problem at all with letting the cords show, but I wanted those ugly cords to be hidden. That involved winding them along individual branches, up and down, back and forth, going up on the ladder and down on the knees, adding cords on top of cords in a way that brought them back down to the multi-plug extender I attached to the wall. While my family watched Christmas movies and drank hot chocolate, I labored on the tree, getting evergreen needles in my tangled hair, evergreen sap on my perforated fingers, and frustration oozing from every pore. What's wrong with this picture?

One Christmas about fifteen years ago I had an epiphany: buy an expensive, pre-lit tree that will last! I bought one that year on half-of-half, or 75% off, the day after Christmas. I paid no more than I had been spending every year for my live trees, and it is still going strong! It goes up in a flash, with help, it comes down in a flash, with help, I can store it in the attic or the rented storage room, and it's beautiful even without any decorations! You may want to do the same. Then you can spend those four hours of not fiddling with the lights watching Christmas movies and drinking hot chocolate with your family and friends.

You will be amazed by how you will accumulate ornaments over the years. Your kids will make them at school. Your friends will give them to you for Christmas. Your Mom will give you some of your favorites from your childhood. And of course you will buy some from time to time that celebrate special occasions or relationships. So don't rush out and buy ornaments! Buy a couple of boxes of the solid colored glass ornaments at Walmart or the grocery store, then fill in with candy canes, or ice-cycles, or red bows, or popcorn garlands. (I DO allow myself to buy especially cute ornaments on half-of-half the day after Christmas.)

One of the greatest inventions of the last few years is the starchy mesh you can buy in rolls at craft stores or at many nice florists and garden centers. You can stuff it into the empty places in the interior of your tree. if you are using a balsam, and it gives you instant fullness. I like to pouf it out in the empty spaces then tuck it back in at the trunk and come out in another empty space. Depending on the size of your tree, you will probably need two or more rolls. In the off-season, you can buy them very cheaply.

Or you can use it for any one of a dozen other things, such as in the chandelier, or on the stairway, or around the front door outside. Oh this stuff makes life so much easier! And you can re-roll it at the end of the season and use it year after year. Between mesh and good artificial greenery and wired cloth ribbon, Christmas decorating has become a lot easier and a lot more fun than it used to be.

THE GREENERY

You will be amazed by how much live greenery you can find all around you – in your and your neighbors' yards, in parks, and out in the country. Live greenery is the most festive of all the traditional decorative materials, but it doesn't last long. It can also be messy – and so it requires special treatment – but nothing dresses up a holiday scene more than holly and berries, pine boughs and cones, and magnolia branches. Just be sure that you snip off the pieces you want to use in ways that do not harm the remaining shape of the bush or tree.

All fresh greenery needs to be *conditioned*, which means it needs to be completely immersed in water for a day or two. This will make it last longer before it starts to dry out and turn brown. After you have dried it off thoroughly and decided where you want to use it, you need to dip the snipped ends in paraffin, which will keep them from oozing sap onto your furniture and table coverings. You can gather little bundles and tie them together on lamps or candlesticks. You can poke them in Styrofoam, or better, soaked oasis to make arrangements for your coffee table or front hall, you can bundle them and tie them to cords to make garlands for your doorways or stairs. Accent them with red bows and you are well on your way toward an old-fashioned Christmas look.

Good artificial greenery is well worth the price, especially if you can get it on sale. (One Christmas dinner we had Canadian Balsam needles dropping from the chandelier onto the table – and into the food – during Christmas Dinner. Oops!) *After* Christmas this year invest in good *silk* wreaths for your doors and windows, on half-of-half, of course. They will last forever. Ditto on good silk garlands for the stairways or to go around doors. Nothing says Christmas like swags of greenery adorned with red ribbons. All through December, notice where the cute decorations and good artificial greenery are being sold. Make notes so you can plan your after-Christmas sale shopping.

If you do go with artificial greenery, and eventually you will, buy silk and **not** plastic, which begins to have a funny smell after a year or two. Use *pot pourri*, or scented candles, or simmering scents on the stove, or some kind of room spray to keep good evergreen scents wafting through the house.

The Smells of Christmas:

2 cups water
1 tablespoon whole cloves
3 cinnamon sticks
1 teaspoon ground nutmeg

Simmer all in a pan on the top of the stove.
Add water and spices as needed

And by all means play lots of Christmas music while you work on your decorations. Nothing will get you in the Christmas spirit faster than that!

Poinsettias provide a wonderful splash of red that dresses up any area, but they also require special care. Do not leave them in the hat-shaped baskets they often arrive in from the florist – the plastic lining of the basket will smother the plant. Find another basket or pot that will allow them to breathe. When they start to droop, take them out of the container, set them in a plate of water, and leave them overnight. They are happier being watered from the bottom, though I do have one friend who drops in ice cubes from the top. Do **not** put them next to a heat register or in a draft – they will not make it; but if you find a happy spot and water them properly, poinsettias should stay pretty throughout the season. When they start to drop their leaves, throw them away!

Live **mistletoe** is great fun but it lasts about two days. Don't bother! Lovely Williamsburg apple trees are gorgeous as a centerpiece, but the apples shrivel and fall off and the holly dries up and drops out after less than a week. Find something that will last! Of course if you are having a very special party that requires fresh flowers, by all means enjoy using them. Otherwise work out a centerpiece that will look pretty on your table through the whole season.

THE TABLE

First you need to decide on a centerpiece. This does not have to be dramatic or large – remember, you are going to want to be able to talk over it during your Christmas festivities. An easy solution is to use a cloth runner of some kind that can be laid flat or scrunched. If you are going to use a tablecloth, two ribbons the whole length of the table can serve as a runner. In the center of the table place an oblong mirror or tray, and on top of that a silver, crystal or glass bowl filled with colored balls you bought at the grocery store and didn't use on the tree. Add simple candlesticks on either side of the bowl, and you have a lovely Christmas table!

The possibilities are endless. One year I did use live evergreen boughs and holly in oasis, in a footed silver bowl, with a few red velvet bows on picks; I watered them every day, and they did make it through three weeks, if just barely. Ever since then I've been using tiny red bromeliads in a crystal bowl, with glass marbles in the bottom and sphagnum moss on top, and those little fellows last for months. My friend Suzanne uses little gold sparkly trees of different sizes on a mirror surrounded by artificial greenery. My friend Dee uses a large art-glass bowl with good *pot pourri* in the middle, framed by tall silver candelabras, and she has lots of Santas marching in and out. The best approach is to use a bowl of your grandmother's and some treasures your Mother gave you surrounded by greenery. They will make you happy every day, and they will be great conversation-starters for your guests.

For good ideas for centerpieces and other Christmas decorations visit the Christmas Blog Network, especially "Little Miss Christmas." Many of the items you'll find there are too glitzy and bling-y for an old-fashioned Christmas, but they will spark your imagination and help you get started.

Next you need to think about placemats and napkins. If you are having a formal Christmas Dinner, you probably need to use white, which you can dress up by tying the napkins with red ribbons. You will not need placemats if you are using a tablecloth. You may also need to stick with white if the colors in your dishes would clash with red or green, silver or gold. If you are fortunate enough to have Christmas dishes, or white dishes, then the sky is the limit on what you can do from there. Once again, keep your purchases to a minimum, and remember that each one is an investment, and that all will have to be *stored*.

Party tablecloths do not need to be expensive, and they can set the tone for a festive celebration. Check out your fabric stores for end pieces or discontinued patterns – sometimes just two or three yards will be enough to cover your table with one seam down the middle. If you cut the edges with pinking shears you will not even have to hem the cloth, and you can layer it on top of a white cloth that hangs down below it. Look for a taffeta plaid that will not show spills, and get ready to have a great party!

If you eat most of your meals on the kitchen or breakfast room table, this is the place to play with color. I use a wooden advent wreath as a centerpiece here, to which I have glued tiny painted figures from the manger scene, or crèche. Then I use red wipe-off placemats and red and white polka dotted napkins edged with green rick-rack. We light the candles at supper every night, and we are always reminded of the reason we are celebrating. The color adds so much to the festivity of the season, and the candles make it magical. Aren't those the qualities we are seeking in this most joyous of seasons?

OUTSIDE DECORATIONS

After you have worked out your tree, your greenery, and your tables, you need to think about the front door. You want to announce to the world that Christmas is coming and you are getting ready! There is nothing prettier than a green wreath and a red bow. Bows on the light fixtures also add a merry touch. This scene will make you happy every time you come home.

Your bows are another investment. Have a florist shop make you some red velvet poufy bows backed with gold, and tell them to leave ample strands of the wire they use to secure the bow. You use these wires to attach the bows to your wreaths or garlands. Treated properly these nice bows will hold up for several years. At the end of the season attach the bows to a coat hanger, cover them with plastic wrap from your dry cleaning, and hang them in the attic or in the storage closet with your wreaths – wherever they will not get crushed.

Outside decorations are a real challenge. Children love them, and they especially love lights all over the outside of the house. If your husband thinks decorating with lights is fun, by all means let him do it! Otherwise, try to keep it simple.

Struggling with lights and cords, sleighs and reindeer, in the cold, causes brain damage. However, in a nod to my children's desire for outside lights I started putting electric candles in the windows, on the inside, and discovered I loved the look. When I added a garland around the entryway and spotlights on the front doors, my outside was done!

THE REST OF IT

On the rest of your decorating, restrain yourself. Remember, you are going to have to take it all down and put it away, and putting it away will take just as long as getting it out. You *will* get caught up in the spirit of the season, and you will want to put charming decorations in every nook and cranny, but add new items with great care. Each purchase is an investment, and it will be with you for a long time. I try to stick to the rule of buying one new tree ornament and one new house decoration each year, and I wish now that I had dated them on the bottom with a paint pen. There is always so much cute stuff out there that we feel compelled to buy it, then we have to figure out how to use it, and how to store it. Try to be very frugal until you know your tastes. No impulse buys!

Choose one color – red?, green? silver? – for your household decorating and stick with that for the year. Remember, you are BUILDING. Don't let yourself go off in all directions or the finished product will have a jumbled feel. Each year you will grow more secure in your tastes and choices, and each year you will be able to add more depth and quality.

Red bows will go a long way in your Christmas decorating, but use good cloth ribbon which you have, of course, bought on sale. Narrow red grosgrain ribbon works beautifully on the chandeliers, lamps and candlesticks. At the end of the season you can put the untied bows in baggies, write on the bag where you used them, and put the baggie in a cabinet in the room where they will be used again. Wide ribbon that is wired on the edges can make beautiful bows that you can secure with tiny wires and attach to almost anything.

My best decoration is the Christmas cards that arrive at my house throughout the season and start marching across my den bookshelves. They make me feel surrounded by the love of friends. Another favorite decoration is the Christmas books we collected while our boys were growing up. I spread them out so the covers show, and this serves as an invitation for people to pick them up and read a bit. When the children start coming, you'll want to hang stockings. If you don't have a mantel, hang them on the bedposts, or on the backs of the breakfast room chairs. Of course, over the fireplace is just about perfect.

As the years go by, you'll collect more and more treasured decorations, and you'll find places you love to use them. Just remember that everything you buy has to be stored. Putting things away in boxes greatly complicates the decorating process, and so I always try to store my decorations, unboxed, in the rooms where I use them. If at all possible, try to clean out some cabinet and closet space that you can designate specifically for Christmas decorations, leaving just the tree and the wreaths to go in the attic or storeroom.

If you have to use boxes for your storage, organize them by room and mark them clearly. The large clear tubs with plastic lids are your best bet here – so you can see what is inside without having to drag all of them out at once. Then just decorate one area at a time. If you bring out all the boxes at once they will become very oppressive, and that's *not* what we are after. Remember, your living space has to continue to function, and we want everyone to be merry.

Finally, get your house decorated as quickly as possible so you can enjoy it. The season is not very long. My advice to you is to have it done by, you guessed it, the tenth. Now get busy, let those creative juices flow, and HAVE FUN!

Chapter Three
GIFTS and CARDS

"In the Days of Auld Lang Syne!"

Giving gifts is really what Christmas is all about. (Of course it's fun to get them, too!) And gift-giving can easily get out of hand as the years go by. We start with gifts to family – siblings, parents, grandparents, aunts and uncles, spouses and children – and then we move on to co-workers, neighbors, children's teachers, children's friends, lunch bunch, husband's clients, the mailman, the hairdresser, etc., etc., etc. Pretty soon we discover that our desire to give exceeds our capacity to do so, and that's when the stress starts to set in. Do not despair! I have some solutions! Once again, the key to the whole thing is PLANNING.

Long before December, you need to figure out your Christmas list. Write it down! Put it in your Christmas notebook! Count how many people are in each of your categories, and then buy in quantity – on sale – by category. You'll be amazed to discover how many nice things you can find on half-of-half (75% off), and certainly on half-price, throughout the year.

Many upscale gift shops put some merchandise on sale at the end of each season, and you can find terrific bargains that will do very nicely as Christmas presents. Don't let yourself feel intimidated about walking into those stores. Put on a nice outfit and act like you belong there. You do! They will not think you are cheap for buying things on sale. They will be glad to get rid of the merchandise, and they will think you are smart. You are.

The problem with sale shopping is that you can easily get carried away. After Easter you will see bunnies and eggs that you think you just have to have for yourself. Be disciplined. You are not shopping for yourself, you are shopping for Christmas presents for other folks. When you find something particularly wonderful, you might buy one or two extras just in case someone pops up at the last minute you had not thought of (and they probably will!).

I try not to spend more than $5.00 (the marked-down price) for the gifts in most of my categories. Remember, most of your category gifts do not have to be carefully selected to fit the tastes of each recipient; instead they can be simple reminders that you care about those folks and you want to add to the joy of their Christmas celebrations.

Most important of all, when you get home from your shopping trips you MUST record your treasures in your Christmas notebook, preferably with assignments for who gets them. Then store them in a logical place – preferably with your notebook. If you do not record your purchases, you will have forgotten them by December, and you will end up buying too much. If you don't store them together, you will forget where they are.

As you begin to review your Christmas notebook in September, take note of what items you have already purchased and what gaps you still need to fill. At this point, do **not** let yourself break down and pay full price for additional gifts. Instead, start thinking of items you can bake or make – tiny loaves of banana nut bread, little tins of fudge or rum balls, felt ornaments for the three, little grapevine wreaths. One year in graduate school I had no money for ornaments or gifts, so I made lots of felt Santa faces and shared them, and they were a big hit! (I found the patterns in a craft magazine and then made them in two or three nights.) Another year my little boys and I made tiny grapevine wreaths to which we tied painted wooden ornaments with satin ribbon – they painted and I tied. I still see them in friends' homes at Christmas, which always makes me smile.

Christmas crafts are fun – and your children will remember them, but they require lots of, you guessed it, PLANNING! Be sure to allot ample time for the preparation and then for the doing. Choose carefully, because this can be a danger area if you attempt something that is too complicated or advanced for your kiddos! On the other hand, when your children are little this gift-making time can be a very special way to celebrate the spirit of giving with them. I remember to this day a Christmas when I was four or five and Mother set the sewing machine up in the living room and made little felt snowmen and Santa face ornaments for her friends and mine. I have no idea what I did that

made me think I was "helping" her, but I remember vividly the warm feeling that I was doing something fun and important with my Mother. Only one of the snowmen has survived, but I hang him on my tree every year, and he makes me happy.

My favorite Christmas gift, and one that is always a hit, is the fudge I love to make at Christmas. It's fairly labor-intensive, but it gets such a great response that I am always happy to invest the time.

Here's the recipe:

World's Best Fudge

4 cups sugar
2 cups semi-sweet chocolate chips
13-oz can evaporated milk
1 tsp vanilla
1 cup butter (2 sticks)
2 cups marshmallow crème
1 cup chopped pecans (optional – I don't use them)

Butter sides of heavy 3-quart saucepan. Add sugar, milk, and butter. Stir. When sugar dissolves, turn heat to high until rolling boil (about 30 minutes), stirring, then lower heat to medium.

Cook over medium heat for 20 additional minutes (or to 236 degrees on a candy thermometer) stirring slowly but constantly with a wooden spoon. Remove from heat; add chocolate chips, marshmallow crème, and vanilla (and nuts if desired). Beat with wooden spoon until chocolate melts. Pour carefully into a buttered 13 x 9 x 2-inch pan or glass dish. It will be hot and sticky! Use a spatula to smooth the top and clean out the pan. Lick the spatula! About an hour later, score with a sharp knife to mark the size of the pieces you will cut the next day (about one-fourth-inch deep marks). Cover with tin foil. Do not refrigerate. When cool and firm, cut into 1-inch squares. (It will take you about an hour to cut the candy, which is amazingly resistant to your efforts, and also to place each piece in a little foil cup and then into a Christmas tin.) You can find tins in all sizes at craft stores such as Michael's or Hobby Lobby, or in the crafts section of big box stores such as Walmart or Target. I like to put a pretty paper doily on the bottom and top, and between each layer if I use a larger tin.   ~ ~ "Forget the Calories"

Here's an easier gift:

Cheese Log

¾ pound mild Cheddar cheese, grated
1 TB paprika
3 oz cream cheese
½ cup chopped pecans
1 large garlic clove, minced fine
3 TB mayonnaise
Cayenne pepper to taste

All ingredients at room temperature. Blend cheeses and mix well with garlic, mayonnaise and pepper. Sprinkle paprika and chopped nuts on waxed paper. Form cheese into one or two rolls and roll in nuts and paprika. Store in refrigerator. I have given this on a cute Christmas plate with a spreader and a roll of Ritz crackers. You could wrap it in colored plastic wrap and tie with curling ribbon.
~ ~ "Little Rock Cooks"

Another favorite gift possibility is an old Southern recipe that is good at any time of the year with ham or roast beef, and it keeps in the refrigerator forever:

Jezebel Sauce

1 jar (16 oz) pineapple preserves
1 jar (16 oz) apple jelly
1 jar (6 oz) mustard
1 jar (small) horseradish
Freshly ground pepper to taste

Mix all together with hand mixer. This will make one and a half quarts of sauce. Pour into 16 oz. jars (from which you have soaked off the labels), and cover the lids with a round piece of Christmas-y cloth and a simple bow.

~ ~ "Forget the Calories"

And of course the classic Christmas gift is a rum cake. Here is the best recipe I've ever found, and I've made dozens of these cakes:

Rum Cake

<u>Batter</u>:
>*Beat together*
>4 eggs
>½ cup salad oil
>½ cup Bacardi Light Rum
>½ cup water (I have been known to substitute
>>more rum)
>
>*Add*
>1 yellow cake mix
>3 ¼ oz box instant vanilla pudding

Spray Bundt pan with Pam, and cover bottom with generous amount of chopped pecans. Pour in batter. Bake at 325 for 50-55 minutes.

<u>Rum Sauce</u>:
>*Boil gently for one minute*
>1 cup sugar
>2 TB water
>2 TB Bacardi Light Rum

Remove cake from oven and poke holes in it with a fork. Pour hot Rum Sauce over the cake while it is still in the pan. Cool for 10 minutes. Unmold onto a pretty Christmas paper plate and enjoy giving this gift. Everyone will be glad to see you coming!

~ ~ June Massey, by way of Eran Pickens

The possibilities for Christmas gifts from the kitchen are endless, limited only by your budget and your creativity. Just remember that presentation is the key, as it is in all your gifts. A pretty, neatly-wrapped package is fun to receive, and it says that you care about the recipient. A gift doesn't have to cost much, but it does need to capture the spirit of the season by being festive and colorful.

If you can persuade your brothers and sisters to draw names within the family, or perhaps just give to the children, you can save a lot of money. Some people, however, (like me) like to give gifts to everyone. I take great pleasure in buying really nice things for our five brothers on half-of-half the day after Christmas, saving them, and then putting them in the mail the next year. I did make notes to myself about the difficulty of this one year, however, and for a while I ordered things out of catalogs to send to the four corners of the country. Here's what I wrote in 1999: "Wrapping and mailing to five brothers' families causes too much brain damage – and takes too much TIME. Have Purdy's [our local gift shop] do it; it's worth the money! Doing it myself means choosing the paper, ribbon, and tags, and finding scotch tape, packaging tape, mailing labels, mailing boxes, and packing materials. Yikes!"

Trips to the post office are also very tedious (especially when it's cold and the lines are long), and postage rates seem to climb higher every year. Catalog orders make a lot of sense for special out-of-town presents. Donations to a favorite charity are also a good solution – and the charity will send a note to your recipients telling them that you have made a gift in their name. I remember one year when I made a donation to Heifer International in honor of our brothers, one of them wrote back "I never thought I'd be writing a thank you note for a water buffalo!" That was fun.

Catalog orders save stress, and sometimes you can get a discount if you order early. One of my favorites, Wolferman's, gives a 15% discount if you order before October 15th. Others probably do too. Catalog companies assess an extra charge to deliver your gifts to your

recipients, but it is well worth the expense when you consider the savings in your time.

If November arrives and you haven't filled in all the blank spaces in your notebook, it's time to consider paying full price, and that's no fun. At that point you probably need to consider some simple cooking projects – *everyone* loves Christmas calories!

Make a chart in your Christmas notebook showing what you plan to give each person, and then what they give you. Leave a space to check off when you write your thank you note. This way you can look back each year to see what they gave you and what you gave them. And you can be sure that you don't give them back something they gave you last year! (I recommend gift re-cycling!)

By December you'll need to have a few generic gifts available, wrapped, in case someone appears at your door with a gift for you that you weren't expecting. Something you've cooked would be perfect, such as roasted pecans, a ring of rolls, or a small tin of fudge or cookies. I can't say it often enough: gifts do not have to be expensive; a small expression is all it takes to add to someone's Christmas cheer. Then after you have covered all the bases on your "category" gifts, you can concentrate your energies on the special gifts you carefully select or make for your family and best friends.

Of course, cheery wrapping can make all the difference in the world to how a gift *feels* to the recipient. I try to buy gifts at the stores where the wrapping is free. If you need to do your own wrapping, here are a few guidelines. Children want gifts wrapped in boxes complete with bows. Everyone else is perfectly happy with a gift in a cute bag with tissue paper. Work out a wrapping scheme for each category, preferably using the cheerful bags you bought last year at the end of the season!

One clever friend I know always wraps her gifts in the Sunday comics section she has saved all year. Another wraps smaller gifts in the brown paper bags from the grocery store and ties them with green or red ribbon. If you have to buy paper, buy the rolls – which make a much prettier gift – and buy just a few rolls of coordinating paper and ribbon that can mix and match. One simple and elegant way to wrap a gift is to tie one strand of ribbon around the shorter side of the rectangle and then tie a simple bow – like you are tying your sneakers. I prefer wide cloth ribbon that is wired, which you can buy at almost any craft store. Watch for it at the end of the season and then buy the paper to match.

Set up a wrapping area that will work both for you and the kids – it can be as simple as a card table in an area that doesn't get much use. Stock it with scotch tape, scissors, gift tags, pens, wrapping paper, and ribbon. Give the kids a few pointers on how to fold the corners and tie the bows, then let them do their own wrapping. They'll love it, and they'll be proud of their creations.

Do not use your bedroom as a gift-wrapping space. This becomes oppressive!

Do <u>not</u> leave the wrapping for the last minute. This inevitably causes stress.

Get the wrapping <u>and</u> <u>the</u> <u>delivering</u> done as early as possible. This will be a tremendous relief!

Here's how to wrap a package: put your gift in a box with tissue paper. Leaving the wrapping paper on the roll, roll out just enough to go under the box and then over it, with about two inches to spare on each end. Cut that much paper off the roll. Move the box toward one side edge of the paper, leaving enough space for the paper on that side to reach, when folded in, about an inch past the mid-point of that side. Cut off the excess paper on the other side, leaving enough space for the paper on *that* side also to reach, when folded in, about an inch past the mid-point of that side. Turn the box upside down in the middle of the paper. Fold the long sides in toward the middle, straighten the box on the paper, and tape one of the long sides to the box. Fold the other long side in, pulling it tight, then fold over the raw edge to make it look neat and tape it.

Now the trick is to make neat corners. With the box still upside down, on one of the two sides of the package that are still open, (and you will repeat this on the other side), press in the shorter edges toward the middle and then mash the top layer down neatly – making a crease along what is now the top side of the box. Holding it down with one hand, use the other hand to fold the bottom layer up, making a crease along what is now the bottom side of the box. In a minute you will tape this shut, but first you need to make an additional fold of the paper that is on the bottom, so you will have a very neat finished product. You will be so proud of yourself, and your package will be so pretty!

Here's how to tie a fancy bow: Tie one piece of ribbon around the package and knot it (neatly) in the center of the top side. Cut both ends of the ribbon on an angle, leaving about six inches on either end. Cut an additional yard of ribbon, with both ends on an angle. Grasping one end of the unattached piece about four inches from the end, with the "right" side facing up, make a twist in the ribbon so that the "wrong" side is now facing up. Make a loop and come back to the middle (with the "right" side being on the outside, obviously), then twist the ribbon again, right above the original twist. Continue to make loops and twists until the bow is the size you want (you'll have to hold it with one hand while you make loops with the other), then tie both ends of the knot over it (neatly) to secure the bow. Oh what a pretty package! Now affix a tag and you are done!

My mother sold gorgeous, high-end Christmas cards in the summers to make her pin money all through the years of my growing up, so I have been sending Christmas greetings for many, many years (let's not say <u>how</u> many!). I used to love to play with her left-over samples – the gold-embossed Madonnas, the flocked trees, the merry, fuzzy Santas – and they must have shaped a lot of my desire to pull out all the stops at Christmas. I have been amazed by how much I look forward to hearing from all the folks I have made it a point to keep on my list – from camp buddies to college chums to former professional colleagues to dear friends who have moved away. As the cards pour into my mailbox in December, I feel a warm sense of connection with people I do not want to lose.

My advice to you on cards, of course, is to send them, at least every two or three years. It is the very best way to keep up with friends over the years, and it will force you to keep your address book up-to-date. You'll be amazed how easily friends can slip away if you don't make the effort to stay connected, and you'll also be amazed by how much people appreciate Christmas cards. (One Grinch complained in the newspaper last year about receiving newsy Christmas letters, but I think he is decidedly in a minority.)

Now, there's no question about it that cards are expensive, especially with the cost of postage these days. Many years ago one of my friends wrote in one of her books about sending Christmas cards, saying "Is it worth it to spend nine cents to tell my friends that I love them? It is to me." Oh my, where did that nine cent postage go? So you'll have to cut back and be selective about the people you want to gift with a card.

I no longer send the boxed cards – they are just too expensive. For several years I had card stock printed with cute graphics and our greetings, and then I affixed a photograph I had asked Walmart to reproduce in quantity. Even with a great deal on pictures – sometimes as low as eighteen cents each if you order 100, the postage and the card itself will make each one you send cost upward of a dollar and a half. Finally I just went straight to Walmart's photo card, because it is worth it to me to stay in touch with people I have loved over the years. Companies like Shutterfly also have great deals on picture cards.

If, after two or three years you have not heard back from some of the people on your list, you might decide to let them go. And I have been known to send only to the people who sent to me the year before. But the real benefit is to me, for as the cards come in I love to read about the fascinating lives that old friends have constructed for themselves.

Another option is to send your greetings by email. Obviously, this will mean you will have to collect a lot of email addresses, but it shouldn't be too hard to construct a separate "group" on your server that you intend to use for Christmas greetings. More and more, I am receiving lots of these, and some clever friends even know how to add bells and whistles such as making it snow on a picture of their house. Someone will have to help me with that one!

If you decide to go the old fashioned route, choose your cards in October and have them printed (you can order these online at Shutterfly, Walmart, etc.). Stuff and address them in November, and have them ready for mailing by the first week in December. You can use clear labels that make the addressing practically effortless, and with a pretty, interesting font they're almost as good as hand-written.

Work up a set of Christmas card labels on your computer and keep the addresses current all through the year. (I use mine as my address book.) Then you can just print them out on clear labels in November and get your cards ready before Thanksgiving for mailing early in December.

Enclose a Xeroxed letter with pretty, colorful graphics – no more than one page. Just a newsy update about your doings that year – and try not to brag too much about your children. Here's one of mine (it would be even better with a couple of pictures – and you can do this on your computer):

~ ~ Merry Merry! ~ ~
(in red and green)

December 18, 2010

Dear Friends and Family,

I was not going to send cards this year, but
when your cards started marching across my
bookshelves bearing warm greetings, I just couldn't
stand it. So here I am with Christmas less than a week
away, with sweet scents simmering on the stove and
sweet carols drifting in from the den, wanting to give
you a quick update from the Watson four.

Tim is still practicing law and has no intention
of slowing down. His "visions of sugar plums"
involve having one or both boys come home to practice
with him in Newport. That's not a likely scenario, but
one never knows! I have spent the year organizing my
house and developing the flower garden I always
wanted. Some of our best hours this year have been
spent on the porch swing in the late afternoons,
admiring the wonders of a pretty yard. We have
plenty of room on the back porch and would love to
have you drop in any time!

In all the bustle and rush of this busy season, my
favorite times are when I stop to reflect on old friends

and happy memories. Please know that you will be in our thoughts over the holidays, and that we send

Lots of love,

~ ~ *Betsy* ~ ~

Now get busy!

Chapter Four
COOKING

"Christmas is Coming, The Goose Is Getting Fat!"

Christmas cooking! Yum! What could be better than homemade fudge? Does anything make your mouth water like turkey and dressing and gravy, or homemade rolls and butter? 'Tis the season when everyone abandons their diets, and good cooks really shine. So come on in and let's talk about what YOU are going to cook for the holidays.

If you are like me when I first started "doing" Christmas, you may be feeling very intimidated by the prospect of doing a lot of Christmas cooking. Don't be! You're going to find it's lots of fun, and you'll get better at it every year. Just be sensible and **don't attempt too much**. If you are going to be cooking Christmas Dinner, don't try to make ambitious food gifts. If someone else will be cooking for you on

Christmas Day, then select a few new recipes and share the results with some favorite friends.

Your first assignment is to master Christmas Dinner. At my house we always have roasted pecans, Stilton cheese and crackers, eggnog, turkey and dressing, gravy, oyster casserole, peas and mushrooms, sweet potatoes, cranberry ice, rolls and butter, and English trifle. Whew! Loosen your belts everyone! There are endless possibilities for this special meal – you just need to choose what your family likes and what you can afford.

Turkey is relatively inexpensive and relatively easy to prepare. Since I did not grow up cooking and had no feel for it at all, turkey was the logical place for me to start (thank goodness my family likes it!). I urge you to start there too, and perhaps you could cook one at Thanksgiving to practice. If you've never done it before, you may want to let that be your contribution to the meal, and let other folks – friends or family members – each bring a dish that you've assigned them. (Or you can just cook no-brainer side dishes and dessert.) As the years pass, you can add other special dishes to the list of things you have mastered, and one of these days the time will come when you can produce the whole menu (if not quite effortlessly)!

Next in order of importance after the turkey are the dressing and the gravy. The dressing is time-consuming and the gravy can be tricky, but these are the two items that make everyone at the table happy, once you've mastered a moist turkey. See my recipes below for some time-tested, family-tested approaches that WILL work for you.

And by all means learn to make rolls – they are the crowning glory of Christmas Dinner, and they can be made in advance and frozen. After that you're on your own – you can have green beans instead of peas, whipped potatoes instead of sweet potatoes, cranberry sauce or salad instead of cranberry ice (a very old fashioned dish). You can have ambrosia or plum pudding or pumpkin pie instead of Trifle. When you find a dish your family likes, hold onto it, and make it a part of your family's Christmas tradition. You'll find that they will look forward to the dishes they have loved in the past.

Everyone in the family can participate in the cooking, even your husband who thinks he can't cook. They can start to master various items, and you'll find that they take pride in their creations. My husband does the eggnog and (sometimes) the oyster casserole, and he carves the turkey. Number One Son started as a teenager doing the Mini Blinies for Christmas Brunch, because he loves them, and now Number Two Son has taken over the eggnog. Someone can certainly do the sweet potatoes, even as a teenager. Little folks can do a relish tray. You'll have to do the dressing and the gravy and the rolls, but you can do all of this in advance.

The secret to making Christmas Dinner work is to do as much as possible in advance and freeze it – I do my dressing at Thanksgiving!. Of course this will depend on the amount of freezer space you have available. The important point is that **all** of the preparations need to be completed the day before, so that on Christmas Day you can simply pop the turkey and your side dishes into the oven and then enjoy the other pleasures of the day. Of course a couple of things will have to be done at the last minute.

I serve Christmas Dinner from the buffet in my dining room, all of which I have set up several days in advance. It's just much easier to let everyone serve themselves and go back for seconds when they are ready, since we don't have legions of servants in the kitchen! You will want to make sure that all of your serving pieces are in good order days before the meal, and that they fit on the buffet or counter. You will need to wash and stack the plates and dishes, locate and polish trays and platters, clean and set out the necessary serving utensils, locate and place warming trays or coasters to keep hot dishes from marking the furniture, decide on candles and greenery or any other decorations for the serving surface.

Here is what **Christmas Dinner** looks like at our house:

Amelia's pecans (make in advance!)

2 TB butter, melted, and heated with
¼ cup Worcestershire sauce and 3 drops Tabasco
Add ½ lb. shelled pecan halves and stir until pecans
     soak up the liquid

Pour pecans onto a large cookie sheet, on top of a layer
     of paper towels
Bake at 300 for 20 minutes, then turn off oven and leave
     overnight
Sprinkle with salt and enjoy
                 ~ ~ Amelia Williams Frankum

Christmas Turkey

18-20 lb. frozen Butterball turkey – move from freezer
     to fridge on **Dec 18**

Dec 24 – finish thawing completely in plastic bag, in
     cold water

Cut open plastic bag it came in and wash bird
     thoroughly, inside and out

Remove giblets – neck, lungs, heart, gizzard, liver –
     and cook (see below)

Christmas Turkey, continued:

Wash out any remaining ice with cold water

Place quartered apple and onion pieces in cavities

Close neck cavity by using toothpicks to secure the skin
over the opening

Bend wings behind head

Tie knee joints together with dental floss

Place in Brown-in-Bag to which you have added 2 TB
flour and shaken, as well as four stalks of celery
to keep bird from sticking to bag

Secure bag shut with the provided tag, and return to
fridge overnight

December 25, early – Remove bird from fridge and cut
slits in bag to vent

Place bird in roasting pan, raised on rack, and bring to
room temperature
Bake at 350 for 3½ hours

Remove from oven, cover with tinfoil or tea towel,
let sit for 20 min

Alert the person who is going to slice that they are
about to perform

Pour juices from pan (or bag) into a 4-cup glass
measuring cup and spoon off – *and save* – the fat
that comes to the top

To the juices, add the liquid you've saved from cooking
the giblets

Have someone slice the turkey, placing slices on platter
on warming tray Keep covered until served,
while you make the gravy (unless you made it at
Thanksgiving and froze it, you smart girl!)

Congratulate yourself! You're about to serve a
beautiful meal!

Giblets

Dec 24th – Simmer all *except liver* for 1½ hours in just
enough water to cover, adding ½ tsp each of
salt, pepper and poultry seasoning

Add liver for last 15 minutes only

Remove from water but save the liquid and store it in
the fridge

Throw away neck, then chop everything else into very
small chunks

Place in covered container or Baggie and store in fridge
until tomorrow

Miss Lady's Gravy

Take giblets and giblet liquid out of fridge and bring to room temperature

Add giblet liquid to the broth that came out of the turkey (after the fat has been removed from the broth and saved)

4 cups of this combined liquid will be needed for Christmas Dinner. You can add chicken broth if needed

In large, heavy skillet melt 8 TB of turkey fat or butter. Stir in 8 TB flour. Mix well

At medium-high heat, stir constantly until tan – about 10 minutes

Add broth gradually, stirring constantly. Will sizzle and thicken quickly

Stirring constantly, bring to a boil (this takes 8 minutes). Reduce heat and simmer for 5 minutes, stirring constantly

Add giblets, salt and pepper

If it is not brown enough to suit you, add a few drops of Kitchen Magic

Enjoy! You have just mastered the hardest part of Christmas Dinner!

Millie's Dressing   Serves 12

4 cups brown bread crumbs (1 loaf); dry in low oven
     then chop fine in Cuisinart
4 cups corn bread crumbs (2 pkgs); use mix; let get
     stale then chop fine in Cuisinart
2 cups chopped celery combined with 1½ cups
     chopped onion – sauté slowly in stick of melted
     butter

Combine above with 1 quart chicken stock and a carton
     of whipping cream
Add 8 eggs, one at a time, stirring well
Add salt and pepper to taste, 1 tsp garlic salt, 2 TB
     lemon juice, 2 TB basil, 2 TB Worcestershire
     sauce, ½ tsp thyme

Should be consistency of cake batter or soup. Can add
     chicken broth if needed

Cook in Dutch Oven (a covered, heavy pot) at 325 for
     45 minutes to set the eggs
Transfer to buttered casserole dish and cover with
     tinfoil
Freeze, then get out 24 hours ahead of cooking
Cook at 350 for one hour, covered with tinfoil
                    ~ ~ Millie Wilmans Page

My Grandmother's Cranberry Ice   Serves 10

2 bags fresh cranberries (24 oz)
3 cups sugar / 3 cups water
5 TB lemon juice / 5 TB grapefruit juice

Boil cranberries for 8 minutes, covered (in water!)
Pour all through sieve onto sugar and juices
Mash berries through the sieve, and stir until sugar
         dissolves
Strain off seeds
Freeze

~ ~ Margaret Cooper Jacoway

Joanie's Sweet Potatoes   Serves 12

7 or 8 large sweet potatoes, cooked, shucked and
mashed

Add: 1 stick butter, melted
       1 cup brown sugar
       ½ cup bourbon
       ¼ cup orange juice
       dash cinnamon / dash ground cloves
       2 eggs
       chopped roasted pecans

Pour into buttered baking dish, top with little
       marshmallows, cover with foil and freeze
Cook at 350 for 1 hour

Christmas Peas   Serves 8-10

Family-size package green peas
Large jar chopped pimientos, drained
Large jar sliced mushrooms, drained
Salt, pepper, butter to taste

Cook peas according to package directions and
        combine all a day ahead
Pour into buttered casserole dish and refrigerate
Cook at 350 for 30 minutes

Scalloped Oysters   Serves 8-10

Wash in cold water 4-6 small containers of oysters and
        drain in colander
In a buttered casserole, make layers of saltine cracker
        crumbs, then oysters, then salt and pepper and
        butter pats, etc., until dish is full
Pour Half-and-Half over all, filling the spaces
Bake at 350 for 45 minutes, until set

Cannot be made in advance   ~ ~ *"Southern Accent"*

Refrigerator Dinner Rolls   Yield: 8 dozen

Dissolve 2 pkgs yeast in 1 cup warm water
Cream ¾ cup butter with ¾ cup sugar; add 1 cup
        boiling water and cool to lukewarm

Add 2 egg yolks and yeast mixture and stir thoroughly
Stir in 6 cups flour and 1 tsp salt (electric mixer ok)
Fold in 2 stiffly-beaten egg whites. Dough will be soft-
        looking
Leave in mixing bowl. Cover and refrigerate at
        least 2 hours (or overnight)

2 hours before baking, roll out dough
Cut as you would biscuits, fold over, and place on
        well-greased and floured pans in warm spot to
        rise. Leave for a couple of hours

Bake 15 – 20 minutes at 375
These may be partially baked, then frozen.

Thaw, brown and serve
                          ~ ~ *"Little Rock Cooks"*

Dorrie's Trifle

Serves 12

Make cake with Betty Crocker golden vanilla cake mix.
Cut in triangles
Sandwich cake with jam – the same flavor as the fruit
you are using
Stand triangles on sides in bottom of trifle dish.

Stuff empty spaces with fruit, then make a layer of the
fruit on top of the cake.

Drizzle fruit juice over all
Drizzle ½ cup of sherry, brandy or bourbon over all
Cover with Saran Wrap and set aside

Make custard. Dorrie uses Bird's. Let it cool until it is
almost set. You want the effect of layers. Pour
custard over cake and re-cover

Chill. Don't freeze. Can do this two days ahead.

Day of serving – add whipped cream to top and more
fruit and nuts to decorate the top
Spoon down from top to bottom so everyone gets
everything
Yum!

~ ~ Dorrie Fitzhugh

Here's how you can make all of this work:

December 10: Finish decorating, put your cards in the mail, finish delivering your gifts, bring your live tree into the house.

December 11: Make the dressing and freeze it (if you didn't do this at Thanksgiving).

December 12: Make the sweet potato casserole and freeze it.

December 13: Make the cranberry ice and freeze it.

December 14: Make the dough for your rolls, cover the bowl with plastic wrap, and put it in the refrigerator overnight.

December 15: Make the rolls, let them rise, cook them for 10 minutes, put the rings in gallon Baggies and freeze. (One batch will make 5 or 6 pans of rolls. Give two or three as gifts, frozen.)

December 16: Buy a frozen turkey and all the remaining ingredients you will need (except the oysters).

December 17: Do any of the above that has not been done already.

December 18: Set up the buffet for Christmas dinner – plates, trays, utensils, etc. You really need warming trays for the buffet. Getting everything to the table hot is a huge challenge. With warming trays, you can say the blessing first and then let everyone serve themselves. The two styles I have found are electric and microwavable.

December 19: Set the table in the dining room. Get out all the dishes, glasses, napkins and flatware that you will be using and set it up. I like to tie the napkins with red and green bows. I also like to make place cards and put little favors at each place, such as little baskets of M & Ms or mints. We like to use the traditional English Christmas poppers that have tissue paper crowns inside, which we all wear. Gussy it up, and make it festive!

December 20: Buy the oysters (if you wait too long they will all be gone). If you have a friendly butcher, maybe he or she will save some for you. By all means keep them in the refrigerator until you are ready to cook them.

December 21: Make the gravy, if you saved and froze the drippings and giblets from your Thanksgiving turkey. Refrigerate. Make Amelia's pecans.

December 22:   Put the frozen turkey in the warmest part of the refrigerator. Move the dressing and the sweet potatoes from the freezer into the refrigerator.

December 23:   Assemble the Trifle (except for the custard) and cover it with plastic wrap. Not necessary to refrigerate.

Assemble the pea and mushroom casserole and refrigerate. (It's getting pretty crowded in there! If it is cold enough, some of these things can go on the back porch, or into a cooler.)

December 24:   Scoop the cranberry ice into stemmed compotes and put them back in the freezer, covered with plastic wrap. (If you let it thaw for about 30 minutes it is much easier to scoop.)

Make the custard for your Trifle, pour over the Trifle, re-cover and refrigerate.

Prepare the turkey according to the directions given earlier in this chapter.

December 25:   Take the turkey out of the fridge and leave it on the counter until it comes to room temperature (about an hour). Cook the turkey according to the time chart on the package, which you have used to tell your guests when to arrive.

Make the oyster casserole and pop it into the oven along with the dressing, sweet potatoes, peas and rolls, staggered, of course, according to the times they need to cook.

(Remember that when you are cooking several things in the same oven, you need to add extra minutes to the suggested cooking time.)

Decorate the Trifle with whipped cream, pretty fruit, and pecan pieces.

Heat up the gravy if you have already made it. If not, remove the giblets and their liquid from the fridge, and when the turkey comes out of the oven – while someone else is carving it – make the gravy from the turkey drippings and the giblets.

Put everything on the buffet and call everyone to the table. Take a bow and enjoy the applause!

Enjoy the best meal of the year, then let someone else do the dishes.

You see, I told you you could do it!

If you are <u>not</u> having Christmas Dinner at your house, you can branch out and try a fancy Christmas Eve dinner complete with candles, and/or you can prepare a wonderful Christmas morning brunch. Once again, the more you can do in advance, the more manageable it will become for you. These meals I serve from the kitchen, since it is just the four of us, and that cuts down on all the hopping up from the table. We do Christmas Eve Dinner about 7:00, after church, and Christmas Brunch after we've finished opening the presents. What a wonderful holiday!

Here's how I like to do **Christmas Eve**:

Uncle Elbert's Eggnog   Serves 8

6 eggs, separated; yolks in blender and blended
     thoroughly

Gradually add 6 TB sugar and blend, then add ½ pint
     Old Forrester whiskey and (optional) ¼ cup
     brandy. Blend (The whiskey cooks the eggs)

In a large mixing bowl, combine ½ pint heavy
     whipping cream and ¼ cup milk. Beat slightly.

Pour egg mixture into cream and beat by hand

In a separate bowl, beat the egg whites (not too stiff)
     and fold into egg-cream mixture

Pour in mugs and sprinkle with nutmeg

~ ~ Lady Elizabeth Watson Luker

Joanie's Beef Tenderloin

½ lb beef, after trimming, per person to be served

Cut deep slits into meat and push halved garlic cloves
into slits

Marinate beef in fridge overnight, covered, in 10 oz soy
sauce and 24 oz Wesson oil

Next day, turn meat over twice, in fridge

An hour before cooking, get beef out of fridge and
bring to room temp

Pat dry with paper towels

Cook at 400 for 45 minutes, uncovered, on a rack

Let stand 15 minutes before slicing into 1" thick slices

Serve with a sauce of whipped cream and horseradish

Twice-Baked Potatoes

6 medium baking potatoes, baked and hollowed out

Add ½ tsp garlic powder

      8 oz sour cream

      ½ cup shredded cheddar cheese

      ½ cup butter

      1 raw egg

      ½ cup green onion tops or chives

Mix all until smooth and spoon back into potato shells,
topping with more shredded cheddar

Bake at 350 for 25 minutes   ~ ~ *"Girl Talk"*

79

Green Bean Bundles   Serves 4-6

Canned whole green beans (vertical pack)
Wrap 1/3 slice bacon around 3 or 4 beans. Fill dish full
     of bundles
Mix 1 stick butter, melted / ¼ cup brown sugar / garlic
     powder to taste and pour over beans
Bake at 200 for 1 ½ hours

                      ~ ~ *"Girl Talk"*

And here are my recipes for Christmas Morning Brunch:

Cheesy Sausage 'n Egg Casserole   Serves 6-8

12 slices stale white bread – crusts removed
1 lb cooked and crumbled hot sausage
2 cups grated sharp cheddar cheese

Tear bread into pieces and place in bottom of long
     baking dish; dot with butter; add sausage and
     then cheese

Mix 8 eggs /1 tsp salt/4 cups milk / 1 tsp dry mustard
     with electric mixer for 5 minutes

Pour egg mixture over bread-sausage-cheese
Refrigerate at least 4 hours

Cook at 325 for 45-60 minutes; let set for 5-10 minutes.
Freeze

Thaw in fridge for 24 hours, then cook at 350 for 45
minutes

~ ~ *"Girl Talk"*

Mini Blinies

Loaf Pepperidge Farm Very Thin White Bread, crusts
removed, rolled flat with rolling pin
Mix until smooth:
2 egg yolks
16 oz cream cheese
½ cup sugar
Spread mix over slices. Roll up into tight pinwheels

Melt one stick of butter; pour into plate. Roll Blinies
through butter and then through a second plate
containing ½ cup sugar and 1 tsp cinnamon,
well mixed
Freeze at least 2 hours
Bake at 350 for 15 minutes (longer, if other things are in
the oven also)

~ ~ *"Girl Talk"*

Curried Fruit   Serves 6-8

16 oz cans each: pears, peaches, dark cherries, apricots,
pineapple chunks, and 3 sliced bananas
1/3 cup butter / ¾ cup brown sugar
2 tsp curry powder / 1 tsp ginger

Drain fruit and place in large casserole
Melt butter and add sugar and spices, mixing well.
Pour over fruit and Bake covered at 325 for 1 hour
Cannot be frozen

~ ~ *"Little Rock Cooks"*

Cheese Grits

1 cup grits, cooked as directed
Add 1 stick butter and 1 roll garlic cheese

Beat 2 eggs in 1 cup milk, and combine with above
Add salt and pepper to taste

Bake at 350 for 45 minutes in greased dish

~ ~ *"Girl Talk"*

Something we like to add to our Christmas brunch is cranberry-orange English muffins from Wolferman's. They are absolutely delicious, and I like to give packages of these as gifts. Somehow I always manage to keep a package or two for the Watsons!

Some Notes to the Cook:

Don't forget that you will still have to cook supper every night even though you are producing this amazing Christmas celebration. Make it easy on yourself and save your fancy cooking for after Christmas. During December I suggest you rely on old favorites you have already mastered such as meat loaf, broiled chicken, grilled pork tenderloin, spaghetti, chili, pancakes and bacon, vegetable soup and corn bread, cheesy potato soup and crackers, and easy vegetables and fruit such as new potatoes, baked potatoes, frozen green beans, canned Italian green beans, apple sauce, and canned fruit.

You are learning SO MUCH that your family and friends are going to love for many years to come. Enjoy every bit of it, and be sure to make notes about all of it in your red Christmas notebook. Take deep breaths and practice your affirmations: I CAN do this! And so you can. Enjoy!

Chapter Five
ENTERTAINING

"And We Need a Little Christmas!"

Oh yes! Christmas parties! This is where the real fun begins. Parties are fun to plan, they are fun to decorate for, and they're fun to attend. Nothing says Christmas like a great party, and everyone loves to be included, so let's talk about how to be a great hostess.

The first rule for being a good hostess is to make your guests feel comfortable. That starts the day you decide to have a party, because if you plan thoroughly and carefully, your guests WILL feel comfortable; with every sense of sight, sound and taste being indulged, they *will* have a good time. So how are you going to produce that outcome?

Successful entertaining depends completely on careful planning, and planning involves making lists. No matter what kind of party you are having, you'll need to think it through completely in order to make it work. You'll need a list of people you want to invite (and their addresses and/or phone numbers), a list of things that need to be done and a schedule of how to accomplish all these things, a list of groceries you need to purchase, a list of jobs for other members of the family or any friends who may be helping you. Use your red notebook, so your lists don't get lost all over the place. Without these lists, you will run off in all directions at once.

After your house is decorated, entertaining is fairly easy – and so much fun! I have found that if I have one party, I might as well have another in the next day or two – say, a cocktail party and a luncheon. You can cook for both at the same time, and use the same flowers or arrangements. An easy centerpiece is live greenery, which you'll need to water every day, in a pretty bowl with red sparkly (fake) berries, set on a mirrored plateau, under which you can twist four yards of red, crinkly cloth. You can't go wrong with fresh greenery from your yard or a nearby park and lots of candles – votives, pillars, or candlesticks.

When you are entertaining, you need to have all the cooking done by the day before, and have the table set. Also have all implements cleaned and ready to use, and if you are serving alcohol, set up the bar. Sweep the porch, lay a fire, clear off the kitchen counters, and clean the guest bathroom. If the children are to be involved, have them pick out their clothes the day before as well so you can make sure everything is there. If you can accomplish all of this, you can be calm and relaxed by party time. It is almost a certainty that things will arise you did not anticipate, and if you are fully prepared in advance, they will not throw you off your stride. Anxious hostesses do not foster relaxed guests!

The best invitations arrive through the mail. Your guests can post them on the refrigerator, where they will be a constant reminder of the party. The invitation needs to be very festive-looking and on a good-quality card stock, preferably printed, or written if you have nice hand-writing, and it needs to arrive at your guest's home two weeks in advance. The invitation sets the tone for the party, so it is worth a little extra expense to create an aura that causes your guests to arrive already flattered and expecting a happy occasion.

You needn't include an RSVP. Most people won't reply anyway! The rule of thumb is that two thirds of the people you invite will come, so that is the way to plan your quantities of food and drink. You can also earn Brownie points with people you know won't come by inviting them anyway!

Large cocktail parties are probably the easiest parties to produce, especially if you ask a few other folks to host with you. Everyone is in a festive mood in the two weeks before Christmas, and everyone is flattered to be included in a great party. The food is also reasonably easy to prepare and serve, and there are few things more inviting than a table laden with pretty pick-up food.

Once again, the focus needs to be on presentation. Use pretty trays, and garnish them with parsley or holly or something that will make them look festive and carefully prepared. Leave the aluminum foil trays and the plastic utensils in the kitchen! These touches tell your guests that this is a real party and that you care enough about them to want to make it special. Try to mix up your trays and bowls – glass, ceramic, and silver, old fashioned and modern – and if at all possible, use something of your grandmother's. Save the wooden and pottery trays and dishes for other parties. Remember that you never serve salty things on silver – the salt will corrode the finish. Arrange the items on your table at different heights; you can use cake stands, tiered trays, or sturdy boxes covered with pretty fabric as bases for your trays and bowls. This is all a part of the fun, and a festive table really sets the stage for a great party.

Place a stack of real (not paper) salad-size plates on the table or buffet for your guests to use. Most folks will graze, but some will want to take a plate. This is the time to use the plates from your good china, or to invest in a stack of small glass plates, which cost about

$1.00 each at Walmart. In today's world of working women and busy young mothers it is permissible to use heavy-duty clear plastic plates, which you can buy at most party stores. Also buy some good-quality cocktail-size paper napkins, four per guest – two for the table and two for the beverages – and place half of them on the table or buffet.

My standard cocktail party fare is chilled boiled shrimp in a clear glass bowl set down in a silver punchbowl filled with ice (with seafood sauce beside it in a small bowl and a shot glass filled with toothpicks) as an anchor at one end of the dining room table, and sliced ham and good rolls (with mayonnaise and Jezebel Sauce – a spicy mustard: see the Gifts chapter for the recipe), anchoring the other end. Small commercial rolls work just fine, and you can hardly do better than those made by Sister Shubert. I then place three trays or bowls of goodies along each side of the table. You want a couple of spreads with crackers, a couple of vegetable-based treats, and a couple of platters of sweets. I like to use cream cheese and chopped black olive spread *(see recipe below)* with Triscuits, garlicky pimiento cheese with spicy crackers, spinach-artichoke pinwheels *(see recipe below – they will vanish)*, store-bought cheese straws *(look for the ones by J&M, they're a Southern delicacy)*, Rum Cake slices *(recipe is in the Cooking chapter)*, and Fudge *(recipe is in the Gifts chapter)*.

Claire Dowell's Black Olive Spread

Mix together at room temperature:
>8 oz cream cheese
>4 oz can of chopped black olives, drained
>3 TB mayonnaise
>½ tsp garlic powder

Chill overnight, and serve with Triscuits
>~ ~ Dee Dowell Buffington

Garlicky Pimiento Cheese

Cuisinart or grate 8 ounces each of American cheese,
>Swiss cheese, pepper jack cheese, sharp cheddar
>cheese, mild cheddar cheese, or others

Add 3 whole dill pickles and large jar pimientos,
>drained and chopped fine

Add black pepper and garlic salt to taste
Add 2 cups Miracle Whip, more if needed
Serve with crackers
>~ ~ Pat Bruner Jackson

Spinach Artichoke Pinwheels

10 oz pkg frozen chopped spinach, thawed
14 oz can artichoke hearts, drained and chopped
½ cup mayonnaise
1 tsp onion powder
1 tsp garlic powder
½ tsp pepper
17.3 oz pkg frozen puff pastry
½ cup grated parmesan cheese

Drain spinach well, pressing between layers of paper towels. Stir together spinach, artichokes and remaining ingredients except the puff pastry. Thaw puff pastry at room temperature 30 minutes. Unfold pastry and place on waxed paper. Spread half of the mixture evenly over pastry sheet, leaving a ½-inch border. Roll up pastry jellyroll fashion, starting from one of the long sides, pressing to seal seams. Wrap in heavy-duty plastic wrap. Repeat with other sheet of pastry. Freeze for 30 minutes. Cut into ½-inch slices. Rolls may be frozen up to 3 months. Bake straight from freezer at 400 degrees for 20 minutes or until golden brown. Yield 4 dozen. Enjoy!

~ ~ Lucy Kay Dulin Moore

Estimating how much food to prepare can be tricky. You certainly don't want to run out, and I am inclined to prepare too much. But since it's all good, my family loves to graze on the left-overs for the next few days, so this is not a problem. My rule of thumb is to expect that every guest will eat two and a half of each thing, with the exception of the shrimp, and you simply cannot buy enough shrimp. A lot of men will stand at the shrimp bowl and eat six or eight, or more, so I buy about four shrimp for each person and then when it runs out, I don't worry about it.

Depending on the size of your party, you might want to set up two bars. I use the breakfast table *and* the game table in the den – this diminishes the congestion in both places and makes the party flow. I also put beer in a tub of ice on the screened porch and wine in the living room, which also contributes to the flow. **Flow** is one of the things you are trying to accomplish – you don't want your guests to get trapped in conversations from which they can't extricate themselves, and if they have an excuse to step into another room they will feel enabled to do so.

I do not pass trays at my parties, but I do put little bowls of roasted pecans in every room and on both bars. My job during the party is to float around and make sure everyone is having a good time. I greet people at the door and tell them where to put their coats (usually on the living room sofa), I clean up spills and make sure the table stays stocked, and I have a good time visiting with my guests. I *never* get stuck in conversations because I always have an excuse to move on, and I have the best time of anyone there.

Another tricky issue is how to set up the bars. Once again, you will have to be guided by what you can afford. A full bar includes bourbon, scotch, gin, vodka and mixers (Coke, Sprite, tonic and soda, and limes), as well as wine (red and white) and beer. I usually buy enough for everyone to have two drinks, though most people will have only one (and a few will have three or four). Your bar can be as simple as a card table with a pretty cloth on it – once again, you are after a finished, festive appearance. I use coolers with ice behind the bar – they're not very pretty, but they are out of most folks' line of vision. I prefer to use real glass barware – one Christmas I invested in fifty Christmas glasses for $1.00 each at the grocery store – I think it adds to the gracious feel of the party. You will need to put cocktail napkins wherever you are serving liquor, wine or beer.

A less expensive variation is to serve one alcoholic beverage – perhaps Cosmopolitans or champagne. A great holiday idea is Prosecco, a pink bubbly drink that is cheaper than champagne. Drop in a couple of cranberries and it looks like a party! Most alcoholic beverages taste better out of glass, and it might be worth the investment to rent some stemmed glasses from a party store. It *is* permissible these days to use good quality plastic glasses – and it sure helps with the clean-up and storage problems. You can buy 6-ounce glasses for wine, and 8- or 10-ounce glasses for mixed drinks. Glass just gives a more elegant feel.

You can make a great nonalcoholic drink using almost any good canned punch with club soda or ginger ale; serve it in a punch bowl or glass pitcher with orange slices floating on top.

If you can afford it, hire a bartender and someone to manage the kitchen, i.e., fill trays, collect used items, and wash the dishes. They should never re-fill the trays at the table – have duplicate trays that they can bring in from the kitchen. This is the finishing touch that will help you enjoy your party. When the party is over, send your kitchen help home with some of the leftover food.

Here's how to accomplish a cocktail party:

<u>Two weeks out:</u>
      Address, stamp and mail invitations
      Plan the menu and the garnishes for your trays
      Place orders with the caterer
      Purchase napkins, plates and barware
      Engage kitchen help and bar tenders

Week before:

       Plan the cooking schedule

       Plan serving pieces to be used – polish all silver

       Wash plates, glasses

       Vacuum and dust, and clean the guest bathroom

       Purchase all the set-ups, ice and liquor

       Purchase the groceries

       Buy extra Ziploc bags and plastic wrap, and plenty of crackers

       Assign times for everything that needs to be done the day of the party

       Figure out what to wear, including comfortable shoes

Two Days before:

       Empty and clean the refrigerator

       Set the table

       Set up the bars

       Remind the kitchen helpers and Bar Tenders

       Cook

Day before:

       Have the keg delivered

       Move the dining room chairs to the garage

       Pick up orders from the caterer

       Review your list for tomorrow

       Cook

<u>Day of Party</u>:

        Have the flowers delivered a.m.

        Place all hurricanes, candles and bows, if using

        Try not to stand too much

        Try not to hurry – you will wear yourself out!

        Assemble and garnish the food trays

        Light all the candles 15 minutes before start time

If you want to be less formal, you can ask each of your guests to bring a dish, but have them bring it ready to serve – pretty dish, spreader, crackers included. Be prepared to provide trivets to protect your table from heat and cold.

A baby or wedding shower is also easy to accomplish. Here's a time-tested menu: At one end of the table – Hot Apple Cider (in a punch bowl, garnished with orange slices studded with cloves) on a big tray with mugs or cups. At the other end of the table – Water in a glass pitcher with ice and lemon slices, served in Christmas glasses. Then along the sides, a Cream Cheese Christmas Tree covered with Raspberry Jalapeno Jelly and served on crackers, Tortilla Pinwheels with salsa, Cucumber Sandwiches, Petit Fours (made by a local cateress) or Spice Cake, Fudge, and Red Jelly Beans in a clear glass bowl.

Cream Cheese Christmas Tree

8 oz cream cheese
Jar Raspberry Jalapeno jelly

Cut bar of cream cheese diagonally. On a glass platter, put original long sides together, forming a tall triangle. (This is your tree.) Use fat parsley stems for a trunk. Cover tree with jelly. Serve with crackers and a spreader.

~ ~ Jamie Darling

Tortilla Pinwheels

1 package flour tortillas
 Combine: 8 oz cream cheese, 8 oz shredded cheddar
            1 can green chilies, chopped fine
            Medium can chopped black olives
            8 oz sour cream
            ¼ cup green onions, chopped fine

Spread mixture to edge of tortilla and roll up
Stack in casserole dish
Let sit in fridge for 2 – 24 hours (to soften the   tortillas)
Cut into ½ inch slices
Serve with toothpicks and salsa

~ ~ Luckett McDonald

Miss Nonnie's Cucumber Sandwiches

Peel cucumbers and slice about 1/8-inch thin
Soak cucumbers overnight in Kraft Italian dressing

Make mixture of cream cheese, mayonnaise, and red
   pepper
Spread on Pepperidge Farm Very Thin bread slices, cut
   round
Layer cucumber slices on top; sprinkle some paprika

~ ~ "Girl Talk"

Mother's Spice Cake

Batter:
Combine 1 cup butter at room temp, 2 cups sugar, 4
   eggs and blend well
Add 1 cup buttermilk, to which has been added a scant
   tsp of baking soda

Combine 3 cups cake flour with 1 tsp cinnamon, ½ tsp
   allspice, ½ tsp cloves
Add flour mixture to batter
Add 1 cup Blackberry jam with seeds

Pour into greased cookie sheet that has 1-inch sides
Cook at 350 for 40 minutes. Cool completely

<u>Icing:</u>

1 box powdered sugar, sifted

1 stick butter, melted

1 TB vanilla

Add heated juice of one orange (perhaps not all if it
gets too thin)

 Add grated orange peel of one orange

~ ~ Daisy Tribble Jacoway

**Here's how to accomplish an easy, at-home ladies'
party:**

<u>Two weeks out:</u>

Put your invitations in the mail

Plan the menu and the garnishes for your trays

Place orders with the caterer

Purchase cute paper napkins (or iron your
grandmother's tea napkins)

Purchase the jelly beans, and try not to eat them!

<u>One week out:</u>

Plan the cooking schedule

Plan serving pieces to be used – polish all silver

Wash plates, glasses

Vacuum and dust, and clean the guest bathroom

Purchase the groceries, and a bag of ice

Make the fudge

Figure out what to wear, including comfortable shoes

Two Days Before:

Set the table

Make the spice cake and leave in the pan, covered with tin foil

Cut the fudge and store in a tin

Day Before:

Peel, slice and marinate the cucumbers

Make the Tortilla Pinwheels

Cut the bread rounds and store in plastic bag

Slice the lemons for the water pitcher

Pick up orders from the caterer

Move the dining room chairs against the walls

Day of the Party:

Have the flowers delivered a.m.

Make the Cream Cheese Tree

Garnish the orange slices for the Hot Apple Cider

Slice the Tortilla Pinwheels

Assemble and garnish the food trays

Luncheons are more work, but they are the best way to get a good visit, and they are a wonderful, relaxed gift to your friends during a busy season. Invitations for luncheons need to be by telephone, two weeks in advance, so you can get an accurate count of who plans to attend. Set your table two days in advance, and then complete your cooking the day before your luncheon. In setting the table you will want to place a knife and spoon to

the right of each plate, and a fork and dessert fork to the left. The lunch fork goes on the outside, and the dessert fork goes next to the plate. The napkin goes to the left of the forks, beside the bread and butter plate, and the drink glass goes on the right. I also put a votive candle at each place, or sometimes I use a little basket of mints. As always, the purpose is to create a festive, warm and welcoming environment for your guests.

My luncheons begin with a glass of cranberry-orange punch in the den, seated around the fireplace, where I also serve roasted pecans and a store-bought appetizer such as Hearts of Palm and Artichoke Spread on toast rounds. My favorite luncheon menu includes Black Forest ham with raisin sauce, cranberry salad, easy broiled asparagus with blue cheese dressing, rolls and butter pats, rum cake with vanilla ice cream, and coffee. The recipes for Amelia's Roasted Pecans, Refrigerator Dinner Rolls, and Rum Cake can be found in Chapter 4. The Palm and Artichoke Spread (or Artichoke-Tomato-Bruschetta Spread) is made by Elki and is sold in upscale grocery stores. The peppered ham slices come from your local deli. I make the butter pats using a rubber mold I found at a kitchen store – Christmas trees and Santa faces – and they are always a hit.

Christmas Punch

32 oz cranberry juice cocktail, chilled
64 oz ginger ale, chilled
6 oz frozen orange juice concentrate

Spoon frozen orange juice into glass pitcher. Fill pitcher half-full with cranberry juice cocktail. Stir until orange juice is dissolved and thoroughly blended. Fill pitcher with ginger ale. Pour over ice and enjoy. Garnish glasses with orange slices.

Mother's Raisin Sauce   Serves 4

Stir together: 2 TB melted butter
                    1 tsp flour

In a separate pan, boil for 15 minutes:
        1 ½ cups water
        1/3 cup seeded yellow raisins
        ¼ cup sugar
        1/8 tsp salt.

Add the hot sauce slowly to the butter-flour mixture.
        Place over medium-high heat and stir constantly
        until it boils.
Add a grating of nutmeg or lemon rind, and spoon
        over ham.

                    ~ ~ Daisy Tribble Jacoway

Yummy Cranberry Salad   Serves 8-12

1 bag fresh raw cranberries, grated in Cuisinart
1 whole orange, grated in Cuisinart
8 oz can crushed pineapples in own juice un-drained
1/3 cup sugar
1 cup chopped pecans
6 oz box cherry Jello

Using top blade, chop bag of cranberries in Cuisinart, then
        orange
Combine above with pineapple, nuts, and sugar
Dissolve Jello in 2 cups boiling water, then add ice
        cubes to make 3 cups
Pour over cranberry mixture and stir until sugar is dissolved
Pour into individual molds or a 9 x 13 casserole dish
Serve in a cup of curly green lettuce, with a dollop of
        mayonnaise on top

~ ~ Marilyn May Craig

Elizabeth Payne's Broiled Asparagus

Cut asparagus to same length.
Place in plastic bag with 2 TB extra-virgin olive oil
                ¼ tsp salt/ ¼ tsp pepper.
Shake bag to cover asparagus.
Broil until still firm – less than 5 minutes.

Dee's Blue Cheese Dressing

1/3 cup heavy cream
6 oz carton crumbled blue cheese
½ cup Helman's mayonnaise
½ cup Greek yogurt or whipping cream
½ tsp coarse ground black pepper
2 tsp tarragon wine vinegar
Squeeze of fresh lemon juice or zest
2 TB chopped parsley

Mix all together and place a TB on each serving of asparagus. This dressing can also be used on roast beef sandwiches, with baked potatoes, on sliced tomatoes, or even with potato chips. Yum!

~ ~ Dee Dowell Buffington

Here's how to accomplish a luncheon:

Two weeks out:
Invite your guests by telephone
Plan the menu and the table settings
Make the place cards
Make the Refrigerator Dinner Rolls and freeze
Buy a mold to make butter pats

Week before:

    Wash the plates and glasses

    Vacuum and dust, and clean the guest bath

    Purchase the groceries

    Figure out what to wear

Two Days before:

    Set the table

    Prepare the den or living room for serving appetizers

    Make the blue cheese dressing

    Make the rum cake

    Roast the pecans

Day before:

    Make the cranberry salad

    Make the butter pats

    Make the raisin sauce

    Wash and dry the lettuce leaves for the cranberry salad, refrigerate

    Scoop the ice cream and re-freeze

    Prepare asparagus for broiling and refrigerate

Day of Party:

    Have the flowers delivered a.m.

    Make the punch

Set out the appetizers and little napkins
Get the partially-cooked rolls out of the freezer
to thaw
Serve the plates
Make the coffee

Another great entertaining idea is to have friends and neighbors over for Christmas carols and cookies. You provide sheet music for everyone, someone plays the piano, and your guests all bring cookies to exchange. You have a fire going in the background and a gorgeous Christmas tree, and everyone feels happy. Don't forget to provide Zip lock bags so everyone can take home some cookies! What could be more fun than that?

You are limited only by your imagination and your checkbook. Informal parties on Christmas afternoon are always festive and welcome. New Year's Day football-watching parties (with black-eyed peas, of course!) are sure to get an enthusiastic response. Chili suppers for the teenagers are easy and guaranteed to bring smiles all around. The important thing is to get together with friends in this most joyous of seasons. Plan it well, don't rush, and have a blast! Merry Christmas everyone!

Chapter Six
TAMING STRESS

"You'd Better Not Pout!"

Even if you follow religiously all the suggestions in this book, the Christmas season will inevitably involve some stress. Our goal is to minimize the potential for that stress and then deal with it effectively when it comes.

The key to your success in this department is, of course – let's hear it one more time! – *careful planning*. You simply must resist the temptation to take on too much, or to make any last-minute decisions. When your house is all decorated and it looks so pretty, you will want to invite people over to share in your joy (and perhaps marvel at your creativity, expertise and good taste!). Don't do it! When you see all the gorgeous decorations around town you will want to try to expand your own. Get thee behind me, Satan! When you visit the stores and find all the amazing things you could give your friends and family, you will want to upgrade your presents for others. Be still, my heart!

It is so easy to get caught up in the spirit of the season and go overboard on the cooking, the wrapping, the entertaining and all the rest of it. But try to remember that you only have a limited amount of energy, and beyond that you will crash and burn. You do not want this to happen until you have all the decorations back in the cabinets and all of the thank-you notes written!

The fact is that there is so much to do! And you want it to be perfect! And you don't have enough money! Try to remember that you have many Christmases in years ahead to master the techniques and create wonderful memories. This year just try to keep it in perspective and keep it simple. It's going to be fun! Really and truly, the only thing that can seriously mess it up is if you are so stressed out you can't enjoy it (and neither can the people around you!).

Another fact is – and there's just no way around this – that women create Christmas and men consume it. Oh, the men may help with the lights, and sometimes they carve the turkey, but for the most part they go to work in the morning and come home at night to a house that is being magically transformed. Those wonderful Christmas elves just seem to be able to do it all without any help from anyone . . . . Listen up elves: it's up to you to educate your men about how things really work around here. If you don't, you can't blame *them* when they fail to appreciate the extraordinary magic you have created.

Along about Thanksgiving you need to sit down with your men folks and take away the remote for a few minutes of serious conversation. You need to show them the calendar you have constructed and the list you are building of things that will have to be accomplished before (and after) December 25th. If you can get them to sign on to help with any of these tasks, more power to you! If not, you need to make sure they are fully aware of all you will be doing to create that memorable holiday for them and the people you love. You will definitely be tired when the season is over, but you *most* definitely do not want to feel unappreciated as well.

Now that *that* is out of the way, you need to get down to the serious business of **managing your time** (because you are still going to be the one to accomplish the lion's share of that ever-growing list). Time management requires discipline and organization, and it is absolutely crucial to the outcome you are seeking – a merry and satisfying Christmas holiday.

After the Thanksgiving turkey has been consumed and the last of the pilgrims has marched back into your "decorations" closet, it's time to shift into gear and start your Christmas routine. This means you must do several things:

1. Set your alarm clock an hour earlier than usual, and get up when it goes off.

2. Review your list of that day's "things to do" over your first cup of coffee.

3. Read a daily advent meditation to calm your nerves and sharpen your focus on why we are celebrating. My favorite little book (and there are dozens of them out there) is *Advent and Christmas Wisdom from Henri J. M. Nouwen*, a publication of Ligouri Publications.

4. Get dressed, and do your hair and make-up for the day. Few things are more stressful than schlepping around in your bathrobe hoping no one comes to the door!

5. Do the breakfast dishes and put them away. At least when your husband comes home from work he won't be grossed out by the mess in your kitchen, and *neither will you*!

6. Take fifteen minutes to tidy the house. Messes everywhere add exponentially to your stress.

7. Now you are ready to get your day underway in earnest. Avoid your computer as much as possible! Keep your Facebooking to a minimum, answer your

emails quickly and do not linger over conversations there, and do NOT play computer games like Solitaire.

8. Make your trips to the grocery store and the big discount stores (like Walmart) as early or as late as possible. In the middle of the day these places are a madhouse and you will waste precious time standing in lines and looking for a parking place.

9. Keep your list of "things to do" with you all day and consult it frequently. It is very satisfying to me to mark things off the list when I get them done. You will also need to move things from today's list to tomorrow's (or next week's), and you will need to have your list with you in order to do this in a timely fashion. I keep a little notebook (with a pen) in my purse that goes with me everywhere.

10. Stay out of the stores unless you are there for a specific purpose. Nothing can eat up precious time faster than shopping during the Christmas season.

11. Do not goof off. At least that's what my generation called it. I think it's now called "hanging out." At any rate, do not waste time. It is not wasting time to linger over lunch with an old friend; it is wasting time when the conversation wanders aimlessly and you've said all you need to say. Give her a hug and say goodbye, then check something off your list.

12. When you are cooking dinner, cook twice the amount you will need and freeze the second half for a meal later in the season.

13. Go to bed at a reasonable hour. Avoid the temptation to stay up late watching that wonderful movie or reading that great new book that just arrived. You will have plenty of time for those pleasures in the dead of winter.

14. Do not drink alcohol, even at festive Christmas parties. If you do, you will sacrifice part of tomorrow's effectiveness, and we just don't have time for that right about now!

Okay, let's say you've done all these things and you still feel the stress creeping up on you. Here are a few strategies for dealing with that inevitable (sorry!) turn of events.

1. Take deep breaths. You will be amazed by how much this will help if you will do it for just thirty seconds.

2. Count your blessings. Gratitude is the greatest stress-reliever in the world, and fifteen seconds of reflecting on all the things that are *right* in your life will do wonders for your attitude.

3. Take sublingual (under-the-tongue) Vitamin B. Go to the pharmacy and ask for it, and they will know what you want. Vitamin B is the body's natural stress reliever, and stress eats it up. Apparently the B vitamins are not absorbed through the stomach, so taking vitamin pills won't help. This is a liquid that you drop under your tongue and hold in your mouth for thirty seconds and then swallow. It *will* help. You probably should buy some at Thanksgiving and have it in your kitchen or your medicine cabinet.

4. Get some exercise. A brisk walk for thirty minutes (ideally outside) will do wonders for your spirits.

5. Eat regular, substantial meals, and don't over-indulge in sweets at parties.

6. Having lunch with good friends helps, but keep the conversation light and happy. This is not the time for disturbing revelations or gossip.

7. Going to uplifting Christmas concerts helps; you want to spend your time doing joyful, inspiring things that get you in the spirit.

8. Spending time in the evenings doing fun things with your family and friends helps. Play games. Watch Christmas movies. Sit by the fire. Decorate the tree together. Listen to Christmas music. Read Christmas stories out loud.

9. Having a massage helps. You may need that little indulgence, so don't feel guilty about spending the money!

10. If all else fails, take a hot shower or bath before bedtime and let yourself relax into the thought that you've accomplished a lot today.

You can expect the Christmas season to be stressful and tiring, but it should also be satisfying and exhilarating. If it's not, you are probably attempting too much, and you should cut back on some of your plans and expectations. You do not have to prove to your husband or your mother-in-law, or your older sister or your sister-in-law that you have mastered the perfect Christmas. That will come, in time, as you learn how to do the things that *you* like. Until then, just enjoy the learning process, and be grateful for all the things that *they* do well. They will probably be flattered if you ask for their help or their advice, and you will be amazed to learn about all the mistakes they made along the way.

If there is one thing I have learned about Christmas – above all others – it is that nothing will turn out the way I expected it to. As my mother used to say, you will just have to roll with the punches. Very little will go smoothly, and you can definitely expect to run into glitches. These are things you cannot control.

What you can control is your attitude: if you can't change it, change how you think about it. Just give it your best shot, be grateful for your many blessings, and have a wonderful Christmas.

Chapter 7
AFTER CHRISTMAS

"On the Twelfth
Day of Christmas"

The presents have been opened and wrapping paper litters the floor, your Christmas Dinner has been enjoyed thoroughly and some of the dishes are still in the sink, the children are hyperactive from the excess of candy and stimulation, and you'd like to sleep late but you have so much to do! Before Christmas the whole process seems exciting, the decorations everywhere look fresh and enchanting, your creative juices are flowing, and the season builds to a crescendo. Alas, after Christmas you are exhausted, you are broke, you are tired of red and holly and all of it, and you want to turn your thoughts elsewhere. But just at that point you have to write and supervise thank you notes, take down the decorations and the tree, record the cards you received and any address changes, and start preparing for next year. Remember, the care with which you do all these things will shape the quality and ease of next year's Christmas. In a word, your discipline is not over!

Start right away taking down the decorations, and try to have it all done by New Year's Day. Just take down a little bit each day, and replace it in its designated cabinet – ideally in the same room where it has been used – in such a way that nothing looks cluttered and everything can be easily removed and replaced (of course this may not be possible if you are short on cabinet and closet space, as most young folks are). I usually leave the tree until last, because I always hate to see it go. This is all very challenging because the fun is behind you and you want to be moving on to other things. But one of the biggest gifts you can give yourself for next year is to leave your Christmas closets and shelves very neat and organized. If at all possible, avoid putting things away in boxes, but if it's necessary, be sure the boxes are clearly marked.

Start with the dishes: all the Christmas-themed plates, mugs, and serving pieces need to be washed and put away neatly. Next come the kitchen decorations. Mine go in a cabinet over the refrigerator. Next come the decorations from the living room, dining room, front hall and guest bath. At my house, these hide all year in cabinets under the bookshelves in the living room. Finally I take down the decorations in the den, because that's where we live and so I leave them up as long as possible. They, too, go in cabinets under the bookshelves in that room.

The last thing I take down is the tree, because it is always magic to me. I feel liberated when it comes down, but I vacillate between reluctance and relief when that time finally comes. Everything except the ornaments goes in a cabinet right behind where the tree stands, and the tree itself goes in the attic.

I am blessed with a lot of cabinets and storage. The real secret to my Christmas decorating is a large storage closet under the eaves upstairs to which I added shelves along both sides, leaving space to store a row of boxes down the center on which I can place my table-top tree (still decorated!). My tree ornaments go in here, and my wrapping paper, ribbons, and books, and the presents I plan to give next year. And my red notebook! Strive to create a space like this.

Clean out your cabinets as you put things away. Anything you didn't use, consider giving to someone else to brighten their Christmas celebration. By all means, if you haven't used it for three years, give it away (unless it has great sentimental value). Give away anything that no longer stirs your imagination or delights you (unless it is one of your family member's favorites). Things that are still in good shape can go into your "give-away" pool for next year.

Make notes to yourself – you'll forget everything by next December 1st, and you will not have shifted into gear for Christmas by the time you need to be well underway. Your notes are essential.

If you have tied bows on chandeliers and lamps, roll the ribbons and put them away in marked plastic bags in the rooms where you used them – so you won't have to re-invent the wheel next year.

This is the most dangerous time for eating sweets. You've been good about your diet until now, but all the sweets sitting around become increasingly tempting. Send little goodie bags home with each family that comes for Christmas dinner, or find someone in your church or neighborhood who needs to be loved on a little bit and pass them on.

If you have to go back to work after the holidays, you need to schedule time for the putting-away -- just like you did for the preparations. Here are my suggestions:

Dec. 26th

Hit the after-Christmas sales early and work them all morning. Obviously, hit the places first that offer their wares half-of-half (or 75% off), then go for the 50% off stores. You are looking for great bargains for next year's gifts, great artificial greenery, and a few additions to your decorations. Also add any tree lights you may have realized you need. Don't forget the paper plates and napkins for next year.

While you are out shopping, have the children take their toys and gifts to their rooms, and

Have someone put the garbage at the curb.

After your shopping spree, clean up and put away any remaining dishes from Christmas Dinner.

Eat left-overs for supper.

Dec. 27th

Make a master list of the gifts you received this year. Record in your red notebook what you gave and what you got; then start planning next year's gifts based on this list.

Decide which gifts you can recycle. Admit it: everybody does it! Just be sure you don't give things back to the people who gave them to you! Record your decisions in your red notebook under Gifts.

Spread out yesterday's sale purchases on the living room floor, and make decisions about who gets what next year. Write it all down in your red notebook. Then box up your sale treasures (and the left-over wrapping paper, ribbon, etc.,) and put them away in a temperature-controlled area (not the attic or the storage room). Also, if you have room, save the good boxes that your catalog orders arrived in and put them away with the gifts – for mailing next year.

If you are using a live tree, take it down, and wear an allergy mask while you work on it. The spores from a dried-out tree can give you sneezing fits and make you sick. The tree is now a fire hazard, so take it to the curb.

Watch a good movie.

Dec 28th

 Start the children (and yourself) on the thank you notes. Make lists for the children's notes – and make a master list of addresses for the kids to consult when they write their notes and envelopes.

Start putting away the decorations, neatly. If possible, store things in the room you used them in. Do not get in a hurry. Do one area at a time and then put it away, so you can avoid the oppressive clutter of having boxes underfoot.

December 29th

Wash and iron the Christmas linens, and put them away.

Take down more decorations. Put them away neatly.

Write five thank you notes.

December 30th

Take down the rest of decorations (except the artificial tree). Put them away neatly.

Record any necessary changes to your address list using the envelopes you saved from your friends' cards.

Write five thank you notes.

December 31st

Take the tree down if you are using an artificial one. Wrap it in old sheets and take it to the attic or the storage room.

Put away all of the ornaments neatly. Repair anything broken. If you have to store them in the attic or a rented storage room, you can buy inexpensive red and/or green storage tubs that include dividers to protect your breakable ornaments. Even so, cushion your treasures well with tissue paper.

Write five thank you notes.

<u>January 1st</u>

Happy New Year! Enjoy the games (after you have finished any remaining thank you notes!)

Fill out your red notebook with your insights and notes to yourself before you put it away. List your needs for next year: more cards for thank you notes? more tissue paper? more gift bags or tags? Put away your Christmas notebook in a place that you can retrieve it easily when you have inspirations or purchase gifts through the year. That's why it is RED – in July you will not be in a Christmas frame of mind, and if your notebook is not obvious and in an easily accessible place, you will not record these notes. Remember, organization is the key!

Throughout January, watch the sales for next year's gifts for neighbors, cousins, teachers, co-workers, etc., and also for good artificial greenery, wrapping paper you really like, stocking stuffers, and holiday clothing items you realized during the season you needed.

Remember to be alert for sales throughout the year – at the end of January, the end of summer inventory, etc. Some of the very nicest shops put great items on steep discount after each season, and after high school graduation. When you find great bargains, buy in quantity, by category, then store your purchases in an obvious location and record them in your red Christmas notebook. If you don't record them, you will forget what you have purchased, and you will over-buy. Remember, the more you can do in advance, the easier (and cheaper) your Christmas buying will be next year.

All year long, be alert to ideas for easy gifts you can make. One year I bought lots of expensive diffuser oil on ½ of ½ and then later found some diffuser reeds in another sale. My gifts to neighbors that year were little green vases with red-and-green polka dot wired, cloth bows, each containing half a bottle of diffuser oil and about eight diffuser reeds. They smelled wonderful, looked pretty, and went right to work in my neighbors' homes as instant additions to their decorations. Each one cost me under $5.00, yet my neighbors knew I had gone to the trouble to create something for them and that I wanted to share in their Christmas celebration. Perfect!

Think about a Christmas card picture all year. The cutest one I've ever received came from a smart grandmother who made her Christmas preparations a lot easier by planning her card in the summer. It took some forethought, but it still makes me laugh. These friends took a beach vacation in the summer with all their kids and grandkids, and grandmother took Santa hats for every member of the family. There they were on the sand in their bathing suits, wearing fuzzy red Santa hats. Now that's a woman who knows how to plan!

Christmas is over, and it is time to reflect. What worked this year? What didn't? Write it down in your red notebook. What do you want to do differently next year? What do you want to try? Write it down! What touched you most about this Christmas? What do you want to remember? Write it down . . . .

As I think back over my own Christmases, I always wonder "What is it that enchants me so about Christmas?" It's not the gifts, because I've never gotten many of any consequence. As a child, they were always practical. As a young woman I had no money, and as parents Tim and I have always downplayed gifts for our boys. We had one gift-orgy when they were about four or five but we found that distasteful, and since then we've tried to be sensible. So it's not the gifts.

For me, 'Santa' does not mean commercialism, or consumerism. He's something much more important – a spirit of joy, of hope, and of love. Santa always reminds me of Charlie, the delightful elderly man who lived next door when I was a child. He had no children, so I became his grandchild, and he adored me. We sat together on his front porch every afternoon while he had his bourbon and a cigar, and he was enthralled by seeing the world through the eyes of a little girl. There was no question in my mind that he loved me dearly, enjoyed my company, and was always glad to see me skipping across the yard toward his house. Oh, and he was so merry! That's how Santa feels to me: safe, loving and merry.

I love to celebrate Santa's coming every year because the child in me is allowed to come out and play. All my zany decorations encourage a childish glee, and each new Santa is a promise that fun is on its way. I think it is this feeling of unfettered joy that I *want* to believe in, this sense that joy is out there waiting. I hope it comes to your house this year, and that it is wonderful. Merry Christmas! May your stockings be filled with all good things. And God bless us every one.

For Further Reading

There are dozens of wonderful "how-to" books out there that can spark your creativity and help you come up with your own ideas for Christmas decorating, cooking, and gift-giving. Here are a few of my favorites:

Bevilacqua, Michelle, and Brandon Toropoo, eds., *The Everything Christmas Book: Stories, Songs, Food, Traditions, Revelry, and More* (Holbrook, MA: Bob Adams, Inc, 1994)

Crouch, Mary Ann and Jan Stedman, *Christmas Favorites: The Holiday Handbook, Decorating, Entertaining and Recipes* (Charlotte, N.C.: The Delmar Company, 1983)

Foster, Juliana, *The Christmas Book: How to Have the Best Christmas Ever* (New York: Scholastic, Inc., 2007)

Helmer, Jill, John Grady Burns, and Kathy Stewart, *Evergreen: Decorating with Colours of the Season* (Atlanta, GA: Collaborators Publishing, 2009)

Hunt, Roderick, *The Oxford Christmas Book for Children* (New York: Oxford University Press, 1981)

Jenkins, Emyl, *Southern Christmas* (New York: Crown Publishers, 1992)

Lyons, Charlotte, *Mary Engelbreit's Christmas Companion: The Mary Engelbreit Look and How to Get It!* ((Kansas City, KS: Andrews and McMeel, 1995)

Robinson, Jo and Jean Coppock Staeheli, *Unplug the Christmas Machine: A Complete Guide to Putting Love and Warmth Back Into the Season* (New York: Quill-William Morrow, 1982)

Rountree, Susan Hight, *Christmas Decorations from Williamsburg* (Williamsburg, VA: The Colonial Williamsburg Foundation, 1991)

The favorite Christmas stories at our house are Truman Capote, *A Christmas Memory*, and Charles Dickens, *A Christmas Carol*. Go find your own, and make them a part of your family's traditions.

Merry Christmas Everyone!

Acknowledgements

I owe my largest debt of gratitude to my three men, Tim, Timothy and Todd Watson, who were the inspiration for this book – and the long-time guinea pigs as well!

Carolyn Schriber talked me through the self-publishing process and cheerfully answered way too many questions. I couldn't have done this without her help.

Many thanks to all the friends who let me use their recipes, especially Dee Dowell Buffington and the authors of "Girl Talk," Kay Brand, Marcia Curtner, and Mary Wilmans.

My Birthday Bunch is my all-time best support group. Friends since kindergarten, these are the women who encourage me in all things. Thanks to Nan Ellen Dickinson East, Jane Wood Hulsey, Suzanne Smith McDonald, Susan Diesel Mehlburger, Lucy Kay Dulin Moore, Jane Ellis Pinson, Marylee Hoover Robinson, Bryce Williams Reveley, Jane Anne Critz Smith, and Ann Wickard Willis. xoxo

Notes

Notes

Notes

Notes

Notes